More GHOST STORIES
of Saskatchewan

Jo-Anne Christensen

LONE PINE

The Publisher: Lone Pine Publishing

10145 - 81 Avenue	1901 Raymond Ave. SW, Suite C
Edmonton, AB T6E 1W9	Renton, WA 98055
Canada	USA

Website: www.lonepinepublishing.com

Canadian Cataloguing in Publication Data
Christensen, Jo-Anne.
More ghost stories of Saskatchewan

Includes bibliographical references.
          ISBN 1-55105-276-8

          1. Ghosts—Saskatchewan. 2. Tales—Saskatchewan. I. Title.
BF1472.C3C572 2000   398.2'09712405   C00-910869-6

Editorial Director: Nancy Foulds
Project Editor: Eli MacLaren
Production Manager: Jody Reekie
Cover Design: Elliot Engley
Book Design: Monica Triska
Layout & Production: Arlana Anderson-Hale

Photos and diagrams courtesy of: Darwin Wagner (p.13, p. 14, p. 16, p. 17, p. 20); Dennis Shappka (p. 37, p. 58, p. 83, p. 92, p. 111, p. 122, p. 130, p. 137, p. 164, p. 168, p. 183, p. 194, p. 197); and the Shappka family collection (p. 46, p. 72).

We acknowledge the financial support of the Government of Canada through the Book Publishing Industry Development Program (BPIDP) for our publishing activities.

PC: P6

Dedication

For my wonderful friend Leslie Charlton,
who told me my first Saskatchewan ghost story.

Contents

Chapter 4 Phantoms in the Family

Chapter 5 Crime and Punishment

Chapter 6 A Strange Assortment

Acknowledgements

This book was written with the generous assistance of many kind people. Many have asked to remain anonymous, and I will respect their wishes and simply say "thank you—you know who you are." As for several others, I will take this opportunity to acknowledge them.

W. Ritchie Benedict of Calgary has once more proven himself to be an invaluable researcher. His facility for finding obscure material is unparalleled, and he knows his way around the paranormal information network better than anyone I have ever met. Ritchie, thank you for sharing your talent.

Vilda Poole of Prince Albert became a valued friend during several months of research. Her self-appointed mission to pin my address on every bulletin board within driving distance of her home undoubtedly resulted in a number of northern Saskatchewan stories that I would not otherwise have had.

Once again, my appreciation goes out to the staff at Lone Pine Publishing and, in particular, to my patient editor, Eli MacLaren. Thanks to Eli's thoroughness and expertise, we are all far less likely to be struck by optical seizures as a result of my fondness for over-punctuating.

Closer to home, I am grateful to those people who assist and support me every minute of the day. Thank you to my valued friend and fellow author Barbara Smith, for providing ideas, advice and the all-important sympathetic ear. Thank you to my wonderful husband, Dennis, who, despite his own hectic schedule, is never too busy to help me with a research or photography request. And thank you to my sweethearts, Steven and Gracie, for just being.

Finally, it is my great wish to acknowledge and thank the people of this province who have so generously supported my first book,

Ghost Stories of Saskatchewan, and shared their personal experiences with me for this volume. You have made such a positive difference in my life, and for this I am sincerely grateful.

Introduction

A few years ago, I took on an interesting project—the writing of a book documenting ghost stories of Saskatchewan. Talking about it drew some strange reactions.

"*True* ghost stories? Isn't that an oxymoron?"

"Ghost stories from *Saskatchewan*? Saskatchewan can't have ghosts!"

The doubters were wrong, however. A few months of research and a tour of the province excavated a wealth of haunting tales. I discovered that grain fields and prairie architecture can provide as creepy a backdrop as any European castle. It seemed that the 1885 Rebellion, the daily harsh realities of homesteading, the wildness of the frontier, and the anguish of rural life during the Great Depression resulted in as many displaced spirits as did the Crusades or the Salem Witch Hunt. Saskatchewan had its own brand of ghost stories, and it was time to tell them. In *Ghost Stories of Saskatchewan*, I did.

Doing so opened up a whole new world. True ghost story books have now become my specialty, and the question most frequently asked of me in interviews is "Have you ever had a paranormal experience of your own?" It's a straightforward query but, strangely, not an easy one to answer. I've had a few inexplicable events in my life, as have most people, but I've never seen a ghost. I believe that spirits do exist, because I've interviewed so many extremely credible people who are certain of what they've seen or experienced. Still, I'm sure that nothing would convince me quite as strongly as actually seeing a phantom float across my living room. Another interesting result of having written a book on Saskatchewan ghosts is that people have since felt they could entrust their own stories to me. Over the last five years, I've collected quite a number of tales from people who wrote to me or spoke to me at book signings. This sequel is composed mainly of these personal accounts, and has been shaped by their unique nature.

For example, many of these original tales came to me in a very sketchy form. I've chosen to dramatize them to make them more enjoyable. But, while I may have added certain details to enhance the sense of character or atmosphere, I have tampered with none of the supernatural aspects of the stories. These remain absolutely true, as told to me.

I also discovered that people who have had a paranormal experience often hesitate to speak openly about it. Many of my contributors have requested anonymity. I have protected their privacy by employing pseudonyms. When you read a story in which I have used first names only, know that they are aliases. In the rare cases where you see a first and last name, it is real, and has been used with that person's permission.

In 1994, I had some nagging concerns that there would not be enough Saskatchewan ghost stories to fill a book. Today, at the conclusion of my second volume on the subject, I feel certain that there are even more spooky tales out there. If you would like to share yours, please write to me care of Lone Pine Publishing. I would love to hear from you. In the meantime, please enjoy reading some more about the supernatural side of Saskatchewan.

Chapter 1

HOME IS
WHERE THE
HAUNT IS

When a spirit remains on this plane of existence in order to continue the routines of its life, the place it is most likely to inhabit is its home. What most ghosts are insensitive to is the fact that their home has now become someone else's castle—and therein lies the dramatic conflict.

Encountering a spectre in a public place might be unnerving, but coexisting with one at home can range from frustrating to absolutely frightening. "Be they ever so humble," our homes should be places of refuge and comfort. Having a resident ghost seldom adds to one's sense of security.

Even those who don't believe in spirits will speak of houses having a good or bad "vibe." But if the very walls of a building can be imprinted with emotions and memories, is it such a stretch of imagination to think that departed residents themselves might stay on? In many cases, it appears that they do.

These tales of wraiths in residence take place in abodes ranging from a tiny Prince Albert apartment to an aging and weathered farm home. In one notable and intriguing case, the house itself is actually the ghost. The tales are diverse and thought-provoking, and bound together by the fact that they all take place on Saskatchewan's haunted soil.

Man in the Mirror

It was truly a beautiful house. But for some reason, no one wanted to buy it.

For years, Darwin Wagner had admired the historic, two-storey, Tudor-style Saskatoon home. He noticed when it went up for sale. And after it had been on the market for an extremely long time, he thought he'd take a long shot.

"The couple that owned it just couldn't sell it," Darwin said, "so one day I just stopped, and I made an offer, and they took it."

Darwin was amazed at his good fortune. Suddenly, he was the proud owner of a gorgeous home with French doors, a huge fireplace, a sunroom, a large foyer and numerous other fabulous details. The only undesirable feature came to light on the very day that Darwin took possession.

"I had got the keys from the lawyer, and the movers were bringing my things into the house," recalled Darwin. "The first thing they brought in was my chesterfield. I was sitting on it, looking around, when I heard my name being whispered. I got up and followed the whisper, and it took me into a back room [in the basement], which was the pantry. As soon as I opened the door, it stopped." It was a strange and unnerving welcome for a man who claimed to have "never believed in ghosts, before that."

Darwin didn't know it at the time, but that disbelief was about to evaporate. Over the nearly eight years he would spend in the house, his skepticism would be replaced with an unshakable conviction that spirits do exist—for Darwin Wagner's lovely new home was undeniably haunted. The ghostly activity was witnessed by not only Darwin, but also his friends, relatives, roommates and a variety of visitors. It was interesting to some, frightening to others, and an inescapable fact of life to the man

When Darwin Wagner purchased this Saskatoon home, he was unaware that it had a history of ghostly activity.

who had unwittingly purchased the house which came with a spectral tenant.

It wasn't long before Darwin realized that most of the phenomena seemed to originate from two areas—the pantry and the attic. The spectre was extremely active, however, and ultimately would go to any part of the house for the sake of attention or a good practical joke. Brisk chills of air would often sweep through the house with such speed and force that they would move the heavy coats that hung on hooks by the door. Footsteps were heard on the staircase, and in the front foyer, the floor frequently creaked as though someone was standing there, shifting his weight from one leg to the other. An eerie, semitransparent image was often glimpsed, scurrying about the house. And it was nearly impossible

"The floor in the front foyer would make the creaking noise of someone shifting his weight from one leg to the other..."

to keep inventory of the items that went missing or were misplaced. Most were personal possessions, but some were practical necessities that the ghost hid in a clear bid to frustrate Darwin. One example was the thermostatic control for the breakfast grill. It had been missing for so long, and Darwin had searched the house so thoroughly for it, that he had finally given up hope of ever finding the device. But mysteriously, after an unsuccessful effort to buy a replacement part, he came home to find the control sitting in plain view, on his kitchen counter.

Occasionally, the spirit's attentions could become physical. "I had a room upstairs on the second floor which was a bedroom, but I turned it into a TV room," said Darwin. "And in that room was a door that led to a stairway that led up into the attic." Darwin frequently sensed the ghost's presence in that room, lurking behind the bedroom door which was always left open. "On one particular evening, I was sitting on the chesterfield with my dogs, and I got that creepy feeling on my shoulder that someone was watching me. And you have to understand that, at this point, I'm living alone in this big, big house. [The feeling was so intense that] my hair was standing up. Then, all of a sudden, the ghost yanked my hair. It just totally yanked my whole head back, then it took off through that door to the attic. My dogs just ran over to the door and barked and barked and barked."

Other experiences were less confrontational, but perhaps even more frightening. There were countless nights when Darwin would awake from a deep sleep to see the shadowy figure of a man standing at his bedroom door. "I think that bothered me the most," he said. "Imagine—when you're half-asleep, and you wake up and you see that standing there… You can't even breathe. You get totally, totally petrified."

The ghost did not stop at trying to approach Darwin when he was sleeping, either. Before long, it was invading his sleep, appearing in recurring dreams. In these dreams, he was able to speak with Darwin, and told him a number of things about the house.

"He showed me the pantry from which the initial whisper came," said Darwin. "[He showed me] that there was a doorway in there. And he told me about a little spot, built in with two by fours, up in the attic, beside the chimney. That's where he used to put stuff." In the dream conversation, Darwin thought to ask the man why he was so drawn to the house. "He said that his family

Darwin Wagner carefully documented the strange images he encountered in his dreams.

had lived there," Darwin explained, "and that he had left to go away to war. When he came back, his family had moved."

According to the ghost, none of the information would be remembered unless Darwin awoke at 5 AM and wrote it all down. "So I got up at five o'clock," said Darwin, "and grabbed a big sketch pad and I let him control my hand. And I still have it here, pages of what he drew for me." The next day, out of curiousity, Darwin climbed the stairs to the undeveloped attic to see if he could confirm one of the apparition's claims. There, beside the chimney, he discovered an 18-inch storage box, built in between the studs. It existed, just as the ghost had said, and was exactly where he said it would be.

The dreams provided Darwin with his first clear look at the spirit that was haunting his home. He described him as "an unattractive, middle-aged male," who was balding and unfashionably dressed in a black trench coat and black rubber boots. The man

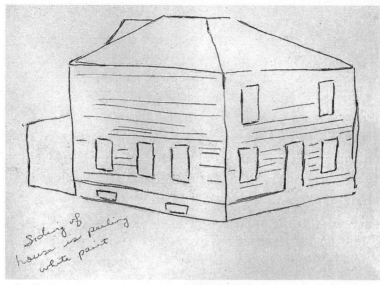

Siding of house is peeling white paint

The ghost proved that it had an intimate knowledge of the structure of Darwin's house.

slouched terribly, "from a lack of self-esteem," Darwin sensed, and his hands were always just hanging at his side. After seeing this unappealing image in his sleep, he was occasionally shocked to see it peering out at him from the mirror of the second floor bathroom.

It was about this time when Darwin Wagner's niece moved in with him. Apparently, the ghost, who had "just sort of been putting up" with Darwin's living there, was decidedly displeased at having to deal with another flesh-and-blood person. The spirit seemed most aggravated when the young woman's presence resulted in some renovations to his eternal home.

"She had been staying up on the second floor in her own bedroom, but she wanted a bit more privacy because she was dating this guy," explained Darwin. "Now, there was a big rumpus room in the basement. And I said, 'Well, I'm going to renovate that, and then you'll have your own private bedroom, bathroom and sort of a living room area.' So I did that, but every time we went to paint or change something, this thing would just act up like crazy. Slam doors on us, hide things on us. And it didn't like her boyfriend ever spending the night. Every time that would happen, they would just get into the bedroom and the door would just slam."

Darwin's niece was the first, but not the last, of the roommates that would spend time in the haunted house. Every one of them had numerous experiences with the ghost, the most common being missing belongings. "This one guy began losing his clothes," recalled Darwin. "He'd be, 'I'm missing sweat pants,' and 'I'm missing jeans,' and 'I'm missing this and I'm missing that.'" Every roommate had similar complaints. According to Darwin, that's when the spectre's activity became the most frustrating, because he felt that he was being blamed for it. "It's like they were accusing me of taking this stuff," he said.

There was one renter who witnessed something much more extraordinary than missing belongings.

"We were down in the basement rumpus room, and we could hear these footsteps coming down the stairs," recalled Darwin. "And he got really alarmed, because I hadn't told him about this ghost. And all of a sudden you could see the image of the shoulders and the back of the head. And I said, 'Oh, look at this, let's chase him!' So I jumped up and ran towards the stairway, and it took off up the stairs. Now, in the kitchen, the cupboards were the sort of old-fashioned cabinets that went from floor to ceiling. And [as the ghost rushed through the room] every door on every cupboard flew open and shut as it went past. Then we ran through the dining room, living room, up the stairs to the second floor and into the attic." There, the ghost managed either to hide or escape: there was no further sight of him.

Various people had various reactions to the spirit, including those who may have qualified as "experts" in the field. Two pastors from Texas, who had performed a marriage ceremony for Darwin's niece, wanted to exorcize the house. A United Church minister who attended a birthday party in the house felt that that would have been a mistake. "He believed that there was not one, but many spirits," said Darwin, who had on occasion seen the apparition of a little girl who was supposed to be the other ghost's sister. "He suggested that… they can be playful, even if they are annoying at times, and become a positive thing in life."

That particular minister was quite alone in his opinion. A priest that Darwin spoke to following a particularly disturbing period of paranormal activity told him never to return to the house. "The spirit's evil. It could harm you in many ways," the priest said. The man's words frightened Darwin, but he felt that he had no choice but to return to the house. After all, he owned it: it was his only home.

Looking for other professional input, Darwin once spoke to a psychic about the strange things that occurred in his home. The man offered, for $250, to spend two nights in the basement bedroom and provide Darwin with an analysis of the situation. Unfortunately, he only lasted two or three hours.

"He came up totally shaken," said Darwin. "He said, 'I've got to get out of this house, I'm leaving. You don't owe me anything.'" On his way out the door, though, he did manage to tell Darwin that he had seen "two shades of amber" floating in the house. That, he said, strongly indicated an evil spirit.

Was the ghost truly dangerous? Ultimately, Darwin felt that it was not. "This thing was mostly a practical joker," he said, "as long as we weren't touching anything, or making renovation-like changes." But he did admit that sometimes the accumulation of "harmless" disruptions could really get to him.

One such day, Darwin was in the basement, ironing a shirt and getting ready to go to work. "I had a big church organ [upstairs],"

This electric organ has played the first two bars of the Bridal Chorus—without human assistance.

he said. "There was no one else in the house, but suddenly the organ was playing the first two bars of the Bridal Chorus. Now, my lawyer had a key to the house, and I had a friend who had a key to the house, so I yelled up to the top of the stairs, calling out their names. No one answered, and all the lights were out on the main floor. So I went upstairs, went into the living room, and the organ light was on. And that was the day I really lost it, because [the ghost] had been playing so many little tricks on me that I had just had it. So I went up to the second floor and I just screamed at this thing to come out, to confront me, to tell me who it was." When Darwin received no reply, he simply finished dressing and went to work. He found that leaving the house that evening was easier than returning, however.

"I waited, I think, until two or three o'clock in the morning," he said. "And when I did pull up to the front of my house, I could see that my drapes were pulled open and someone was standing in the front window, looking at me." Despite his impulse to leave, Darwin went inside, built a roaring fire, and even sat down at the organ to play a few hymns. "I knew that if I didn't play it then, I'd never play it again," he remembered. The remainder of the night was uneventful.

In 1993, Darwin sold the house. Once again, it sat on the market for quite a long time. During that period, the real estate agent scheduled an open house. One woman who attended the event admitted that she wasn't interested in buying, but was interested in looking around, because she had lived there a long time ago when the house was used as a nursing residence. Eventually, she said to Darwin, "I have to tell you a story."

"There used to be, up in the second-floor bathroom, a mirror in the shape of Saskatchewan over the sink," the woman said. Darwin told her that the unusual glass was still there, and the woman continued. "Well, every time the girls would go into the bathroom, this bald-headed guy dressed in black would be looking at us from that mirror." Darwin immediately went to get his sketches of the ghost. When the woman looked at them, she didn't hesitate. "That's him," she said. "Same guy."

Eventually the house did sell, and Darwin invited a crowd of his friends over for one final party. "There were probably 20 of us sitting around in the living room," he explained, "and I was telling them the story about the ghost, and my dreams, and the drawings that I made of the secret doorway in the pantry. And all the big macho guys are going, 'Oh, you're so full of shit.' I told them, 'This is what happened. All I can do is tell you.'"

The disbelievers asked permission to go down to the pantry and look around. Darwin told them to go ahead. "So they went down to the room and they searched and they searched and they searched, and about half an hour later, they came back up and their faces were white," he recalled. The men were asking for a pickaxe. They told Darwin that they had moved one set of shelving out of the pantry, and had discovered a cemented doorway. "The house was already sold, though," said Darwin, "so I couldn't allow them to do any damage to it." Nevertheless, one more of the spirit's stories had been confirmed.

Darwin Wagner had felt that disclosing his knowledge about the ghost to the prospective buyers was the decent thing to do. Fortunately, the information did no damage to the deal. Later on, Darwin's honesty at the time of the sale even afforded him one small luxury. When he became curious about whether or not the ghost continued to be active, he had no qualms about calling to ask. The new owner's answer? The spectre remained very active, particularly in the basement.

It would appear that the balding man in black has no intention of leaving his haunt. As for Darwin Wagner, he's just pleased that his current home seems to have no supernatural features whatsoever.

The Noisy Farmhouse

It was 1976, and after years of working in Ontario, a young woman named Donna was happy to be moving back to her home town of Regina. Donna's parents and sister were no longer living there, but she loved the familiar surroundings and the opportunity to re-connect with old friends. Also, her grandparents, with whom she had remained close, lived just a short drive away, on a farm near Southey.

Once Donna had settled into her new job and apartment, she arranged to visit her grandparents for a weekend. It was a crisp fall day, and as Donna drove her car north under a seamless dark blue sky, she realized how much she had missed this world of her childhood.

"It felt so good to see all these familiar landmarks," she explained, "and to know that soon I would be sitting in my Grandma's kitchen with a mug of tea. All the years I'd been down east, I never knew how much I missed home. I guess I didn't let myself know, because I could rarely afford to come back and visit."

Later that afternoon, as Donna basked in the warmth of her beloved grandparents' company, she resolved to make up for lost time. She would now visit often, and do what she could to help the elderly couple with the house and garden. Because she lived so close, she reasoned that nothing could stand in her way. By 2 AM the following morning, she was reconsidering.

After an evening of conversation and too many home-baked treats, Donna had been sleepy and content. She said her good-nights and retired to the small bedroom across the hall from her grandparents' room. She changed into a nightshirt and settled comfortably into the bed, which she remembered sometimes sleeping in as a child. She would later estimate that she was asleep within minutes—just before 10 PM. Two hours later, as midnight approached, she awoke with a jolt.

"I remember that by the time I opened my eyes, I was already on my knees in the middle of the bed," Donna recalled. "At first I wasn't sure what had scared me, but within a few seconds it started again."

"It" was a loud, sharp, knocking sound, coming from the wall directly above the head of Donna's bed. Clearly, there was no one else in the room, so Donna peered cautiously out the window to see if something outside the house might be creating the noisy effect. By the full light of a harvest moon, she saw nothing. The rapping continued, off and on, for about 10 minutes. When it stopped, it was another half-hour before Donna felt calm enough to go back to bed, and some time after that before she drifted off to sleep. She should hardly have bothered, though, for at 2 AM, she was awakened once more.

"This time, the hammering sounded like it was coming from the hallway outside my room," she said. "I summoned up my courage to take a look, and when I put my hand on the doorknob, it was actually vibrating from the sound. But there was nothing in the hallway to explain the noise."

Donna spent most of the night trying in vain to find the source of the racket, which moved from the hall to the bathroom and finally into the kitchen. At first she couldn't understand why her grandparents' sleep had not been disturbed, but eventually reasoned that because they were both somewhat deaf and were taking various medications, they weren't as easily roused. By the time the sun's reassuring rays began to penetrate the gauzy kitchen curtains, Donna had resolved not to tell her grandparents about her night's adventure. The knocking sounds were disconcerting, but they did not seem dangerous. She felt it best not to frighten the elderly couple, particularly when she had no explanation for what she had heard. Donna kept her secret and drove back to Regina later in the day, where she enjoyed a long, undisturbed night's sleep.

Two weeks later, Donna drove up to the Southey farm again. She was somewhat apprehensive about the mysterious nocturnal noises, but tried to convince herself that it had either been her imagination or at most a one-time occurrence. By three o'clock the following morning, as she put a pillow over her ears to drown out the sound of banging on her ceiling, she knew she was wrong.

"I finally understood that it was going to happen every time, and I started to plan for it," said Donna. "I bought these industrial earplugs that blocked out a lot of sound, and they helped quite a bit. I also got into the habit of keeping a little bottle of Kahlua in my overnight case. If I had a bit of that at bedtime, I seemed to sleep more deeply."

For the most part, these measures helped, and Donna was able to enjoy many weekends at the farm. She was grateful for that time, for in the early 1980s her grandfather passed away. Not long after, Donna's grandmother sold the farm and, because of health concerns, moved into an extended care facility in Regina. There, Donna visited often, but things weren't the same. The older woman's memory had deteriorated to the point where she sometimes did not even recognize her devoted granddaughter. She had her occasional lucid moments, however, and Donna remembers one of them well.

"We were sitting in this lounge area that they had in the home, and I was so sad, because Grandma had been out of it all day. Then when I was talking about the weekends we used to spend together, she looked at me, and suddenly her eyes were real clear. She said, 'Grandad and I never understood how you were able to sleep around that noisy ghost. We were used to it, but we figured it would wake you up for sure.'"

It was the briefest moment of clarity, after which the elderly woman slipped back into her vague fog. In that moment, however, Donna learned a great deal. Her grandparents had never mentioned the noisy entity to her, just as she had never mentioned it to them. But all the while, everyone had been aware of what was impossible to ignore: the little farmhouse near Southey had most certainly been haunted.

Haunt for Sale

The first thing that Tim and Andrea noticed about the house was that it needed a little "TLC."

"The place had been rented out for quite a few years," Andrea later explained, "and each tenant let it get a little more run down. But when we looked at it, it looked like a home."

In 1983, a home was exactly what the newlyweds were looking for. After several years of apartment living in Saskatoon, they wanted to enjoy a bit of privacy and a small yard. The rent on the little two-bedroom place was affordable, and the thought of doing a few home repairs was actually appealing, particularly when the couple saw the potential of the house.

The post-war bungalow had a lot of hidden charm. Behind a tangle of weeds in the overgrown yard were built-in window boxes and a neglected exterior of Spanish-style stucco and brick. Inside, peeling paint and layers of dust masked coved ceilings, arched doorways and hardwood floors. The day that Tim and Andrea viewed the house was overcast and gloomy, making the little abode look all the more shabby.

"The landlord was showing us around the place, and we liked it, but we didn't love it," explained Tim. "But as we passed through the living room on our way out, there was a break in the clouds, and sunlight just came streaming through the front windows. For a few seconds, we were able to envision how cheerful the house could look." Those few seconds closed the deal: before they drove away, Tim and Andrea wrote out a cheque for the landlord.

In the two weeks before they officially moved in, the couple spent every free moment preparing their new home. They washed windows until they sparkled and polished floors until the wood gleamed. Walls were scraped, sanded and painted in warm, inviting hues. The yard was mowed into submission, and Tim filled the bed of his pickup truck with thistles and weeds to be hauled away. Finally, they were ready to move into the house. And the house seemed equally ready for them.

"The last day of the month fell on a weekday," Tim explained, "so by the time we had finished work and our helpers showed up and we put the first load in the truck, it was dark outside. When we pulled up to the house, it was nice to see a few lights on." Outside, the porch lamp glowed warmly. Inside, the hall and kitchen lights shone so that no one had to stumble around in the shadows looking for a switch. It was assumed that they had the landlord to thank for the welcoming gesture, and a few days later Andrea did just that. The man's reaction was a little strange, as Andrea recalled.

"He just looked confused." It was a mystery, but a rather small one, easily forgotten.

For the next two years Tim and Andrea lived happily in their little rental house. They continued to care for it well, planting roses by the front walk and filling the window boxes with colourful pansies. The dilapidated backyard garden shed was shored up and given a bright coat of paint. In a second-hand shop, they found lace curtains for the windows and a pair of huge, old, wooden bookcases. The bookcases went into the sunny loft, along with two overstuffed chairs and a vast collection of books. The young couple thoroughly enjoyed their home, although, every so often, they would puzzle over some strange occurrence.

"It was always something small—but weird," said Andrea, recalling a few of the incidents.

On one occasion, Tim had gone to bed and left a nearly full carton of milk sitting on the kitchen counter. The next morning he cursed his forgetfulness, thinking he would have to pour the spoiled milk down the drain. When he touched the carton, however, he was shocked to find it as cold as if it had been refrigerated. "The rest of the kitchen was comfortably warm. It was *July*," Tim later said. But the milk was properly chilled. It was one of many small, helpful gestures that mystified the couple.

Several times, when both husband and wife were working long hours and neglecting the housework, they would come home and find that the dust on the furniture had vanished. And, as on the night they moved in, it was not uncommon to arrive home after dark and see a welcoming light shining through the window. Tim and Andrea slowly came to accept that they were sharing their home with a spirit, but weren't the least bit upset by the idea. "How could we be?" asked Andrea. "I mean, it did *housework*."

When the ghost wasn't lending a helping hand, it kept a fairly low profile. There were times when the floor would creak, as though someone was walking from the front of the house to the back. Occasionally, the couple would hear water running—but upon investigation, they would find the sinks and tub completely dry. And on one memorable evening, Andrea saw their spectre.

"It was fairly close to midnight, and I had gotten out of bed to use the bathroom," she recalled. "Tim was sleeping and the house was totally quiet. Everything seemed peaceful, but something made me check the living room before I went back to bed. I was standing in the hall, just glancing through the doorway, when I saw the most amazing thing. It was this dense white shape—like concentrated light, except it didn't illuminate anything around it. It was about the size of a human being… just the most incredible thing I've ever seen."

As Andrea watched, the shape appeared to settle into an easy chair by the front window. Then, with a sigh—Andrea still isn't sure whether she heard it or felt it—the apparition seemed to "fold into itself" and vanish. Andrea wasn't frightened or even unnerved by the experience. The truth was that the light form left her feeling calm, warm and protected.

But apparently the spirit could not protect its roommates from what was to come.

About two months after Andrea's midnight meeting with the ghost, she and Tim received some unwelcome news from their landlord. The man would soon be retiring, and had decided to sell the rental house to finance his plans. Knowing that Tim and Andrea loved the place, he gave them the first option to purchase it, and a month to make their decision. The couple thanked him for the opportunity. Once the landlord left, however, they sank into depression.

"We barely even considered it," said Andrea, "because we didn't think it possible. Tim and I both still had student loan payments, vehicle payments… we didn't think there was any way that we could handle a mortgage. Plus, we had very little money in the bank, so there was nothing for a down payment. We were sure that someone else would buy the house and we'd have to move."

The couple saw no point in teasing themselves with an unattainable fantasy, so they quickly admitted defeat to one another. They resigned themselves to the fact that they would soon be looking for another home, and went to bed that night in a cloud of gloom. The next morning, however, it was obvious that someone thought they had given up too easily, for there, on the kitchen table, sat a pad of paper and a calculator. These things were always kept tucked away in a kitchen drawer, and the table had been left bare the night before. Tim and Andrea could hardly believe their eyes.

"It was pretty obvious," said Tim. "We were being encouraged to give it a try." And so, they did.

Over the next few days, the couple went over their budget in excruciating detail. They were able to save a few dollars here and there, but nothing significant. It was apparent that if they wanted to buy the house, they would have to be far more creative. Fortunately, they had some help in that department.

During that time of creative problem solving, Tim often felt compelled to spend time in the basement of the house. It was only roughly finished, and the couple used it for little more than laundry and storage. Day after day, however, Tim found himself wandering around down there—looking for what, he did not know. "Then it hit me," Tim recalled, "that it wouldn't take too much to turn the basement into an apartment." A tenant, he knew, would greatly ease the burden of a mortgage payment.

In that same week, the door of the old single-stall garage became stubbornly stuck. It took several days to fix, and all the while Andrea's Toyota remained trapped inside. By the time the repair was done, however, the couple had realized that they were able to manage quite well with only one vehicle. Selling the car would rid them of one payment and give them a little extra cash.

"For a couple of weeks there, it was like we had some 'force' showing us alternative ways to make this work," said Andrea. "At the time, we never said anything, not even to each other, but we were both sure that it was our ghost. He wanted us to stay."

The ghost got his way: by the third week of the month, Tim and Andrea had made an appointment at the bank. They went in with a sound financial plan and a bit of a down payment, and were preapproved for a mortgage. Delighted, they called their landlord with the good news. A price was agreed upon fairly quickly, and the wheels of real estate law were set in motion. The sale went off without a hitch, and a few weeks later Tim and Andrea took legal possession of the house that they had loved for more than two years.

They invited their former landlord over to toast the occasion with a bottle of good wine. The man happily accepted. During the course of the evening, Tim asked the man when it was that he had first purchased the house, and from whom. The question was intended as no more than small talk, but the former landlord's answer stunned both Tim and Andrea.

"He told us that he never bought the house," said Andrea. "He had inherited it, from his brother, who had been a real estate agent. He told us that he had tried to live in the place himself at first, but that it was too difficult to live in his brother's home so soon after he had died. He always had the strange feeling that his brother was right around the corner, or in the next room. So he started renting it out."

Tim and Andrea said nothing to their guest that evening, but from that point forward they felt sure that they knew the identity of their ghost.

It was perhaps to be expected that there was very little paranormal activity in the home after that. "There were a few little things in the weeks after the sale," said Tim, "but nothing memorable. Nothing compared to what had happened before. And then, eventually, it just stopped. One morning, we realized that it had been ages since anything had happened. It was just obvious that our ghost was gone."

Tim and Andrea felt that, having closed the deal, their phantom realtor saw no reason to stay. Whether he is now resting peacefully, or has decided to move on to another listing, is unknown. But one thing is certain: a spirit so helpful would be quite welcome in most homes. Some would even call it a selling feature.

The Unwanted Housemother

In 1987, two friends named Roger and Sean were 20 years old. Yearning for a bit of independence, they moved out of their parents' Prince Albert homes and into a tiny basement apartment that they had rented. The two viewed the move as the first step in a fantastic adventure. They were right—but had no idea exactly what kind of adventure they were in for.

The damp, two-bedroom suite was filled with a few pieces of threadbare, second-hand furniture and decorated in time-honoured, college-student style. Bookcases were made out of packing crates. The small living room was dominated by a massive stereo system and stacks of CDs. In the dinette, Roger and Sean parked their mountain bikes: it worked out rather well, considering they had no kitchen table or chairs and only seven mismatched pieces of cutlery. The final decorating touch had been a change of window dressing. The roommates had removed the feminine, floral-print curtains that had been hanging over the living room window and replaced them with a gaudy, Mexican blanket. The final effect was ugly, unpleasant and cramped, but Roger and Sean saw a place where they could live by their own rules.

The morning after they moved in, Roger was the first one out of bed. As he ambled to the tiny galley kitchen for his customary morning cola, he saw that some of the previous evening's work had come undone. The Mexican blanket that had been covering the living room window had fallen to the floor. Strangely, it had fallen to the floor on the opposite side of the room, but Roger didn't think too much of it. He grabbed a handful of sturdy nails and, using his boot heel as a hammer, attached the blanket more securely to the wall above the window. He then showered, dressed and went off to work his shift at a convenience store, motivated by the thought of a half-price breakfast burrito.

When Roger returned home that evening, he found Sean sitting on their ancient sofa, studying. He looked up from his books and remarked, "You should have told me that you liked the girly curtains." When Roger asked him what he meant, Sean seemed irritated and didn't reply. Eventually, convinced that Roger really didn't know what he was talking about, Sean did explain. He said that when he crawled out of bed, hours after Roger had left the apartment, he found the Mexican blanket stuffed behind the sofa and the floral curtains back on the rod. Naturally he assumed that Roger had been responsible. Roger shook his head slowly and examined the wall behind the curtain rod. Every nail he had hammered remained in place. A few still held colourful threads of the blanket that had been torn away.

The roommates left the curtains where they were for a few days, but thought it best to replace them with the blanket by the following Saturday, when a few friends were expected for a housewarming party. The friends arrived, and, two flats of beer and several hours later, the apartment cleared out and Roger and Sean fell into a drunken slumber. The alcohol must have helped them sleep soundly, for the next afternoon they couldn't believe that they had remained unconscious through what had happened.

The blanket had been torn from the window once more. It now sat in the middle of the living room, tied in a bundle around the dozens of empty beer cans that had littered the apartment hours earlier. Although it was November, every window in the place had been opened fully. Ostensibly, it was done to clear the stale, hazy air, for the overflowing ashtrays had been dumped and broken in the kitchen sink in a clear sign of disapproval. Finally, all seven mismatched pieces of cutlery had been taken from the drawer, bent into bizarre shapes and lined up on the counter top. Roger and Sean had not said the words out loud before then, but as they looked at the evidence, they were forced to admit that they had a ghost.

Perhaps the worst of it was that they had a cranky ghost who clearly disapproved of their decorating choices and lifestyle. The friends had been anxious to leave home because of rules and restrictions, but now found themselves in an even more frustrating situation. Roger realized that they would never live peacefully in the apartment until they knew what their spectre expected of them. In a moment of inspiration, he decided to borrow his cousin's Ouija board.

Roger and Sean set the board up in the living room one evening. They lighted candles to create an appropriate atmosphere, then sat across from one another and placed their fingers on the planchette. Several times, they asked to speak to the spirit who was living in their apartment. Several times, they received no answer. For 20 long minutes they sat, until their hands began to ache. Then, as they were about to give up, the planchette jolted out from beneath their fingers, slid over the word "hello," and fell off the board. Contact had been made.

The roommates set the planchette back on the board, repositioned their fingers, and asked the spirit's name. Four letters were pointed out: "H-A-Z-L." When Roger asked if this was the spirit that had been so active in their apartment, the word "MAD" was spelled out repeatedly. It appeared that "Hazl" was not quite over the temper tantrum.

Over the course of an hour, Roger and Sean asked the spirit to help them understand what it wanted. They were told, "NO PRTIES," "CLEAN" and "MY FLOWRS," which they interpreted to be a request for the floral curtains. The roommates then attempted to negotiate with their ghost, offering to leave the curtains and keep the apartment relatively clean. In return they asked if the occasional party would be all right, as long as they promised to clean and air the rooms the next day. There was a long pause. The planchette then dragged across the board to the word "Goodbye." It would not budge after that.

It appeared that a deal had been made. Roger and Sean did their best to honour their part of it—but when they did slip, on occasion, there would be a stern reminder from their resident ghost. Often, it took the form of water poured into their shoes.

As for the spectre's identity, she hadn't been lying. As time went on, Roger and Sean received the odd piece of junk mail addressed to a former tenant, an elderly woman named Hazel, who had moved from the apartment into an extended care home shortly before her death. The woman's spirit must have returned to the apartment, expecting it to be just as she left it. Although it wasn't, she must have been reasonably content to end up with two living roommates who were willing to follow her rules. The afterlife may not have been perfect for Hazel, but at least she was no longer constantly "MAD."

Ghosts In Them Thar Hills

Despite being a province that is noted for its flat prairie landscape, Saskatchewan actually boasts many areas of beautiful, rolling hills. Jeannie and Todd were a couple on vacation several years ago when they found one such scenic area. And because of their sharp eyes and open minds, they discovered something even more interesting than scenery.

"We had just started driving for the day, so I know we weren't seeing things because of fatigue or highway hypnosis," stressed Todd. "This was about ten o'clock in the morning, and we were really very fresh and alert."

The two had been driving for only an hour or two when they crested a hill. Before them lay a particularly beautiful valley, filled with well-tended fields, gorgeous groves of trees and the winding ribbon of road. In the midst of the breathtaking scene was a farmyard with a smartly painted white house, a number of tidy outbuildings, and a bright red and white barn.

"I noticed the farmyard," said Jeannie, "because it was really something to admire. So well kept. I was glad to see that the road would be taking us directly by it, because I wanted a closer look."

Jeannie and Todd drove on, winding their way through the lovely area. There were many small peaks and dips in the road, but when the car began a steeper, steadier climb, Jeannie realized that they were leaving the valley. She also realized that she had not seen the idyllic farm setting for which she had been watching.

"It made no sense to me, because when I had looked down and first seen it, it was right by the side of the road that we were

A couple on vacation discovered that there is more than what meets the eye in some of Saskatchewan's lovely scenery.

travelling on," said Jeannie. "I asked Todd, 'Did we pass a white house back there?' He said, 'no,' and I said, 'Well, turn around, I want to go back.'"

The couple had no particular schedule to keep, so Todd obliged. The two drove through the pretty valley once more. When they came out on the other side, they could see the bright white house down in the valley. From Todd's and Jeannie's vantage point high atop the hill, it was obvious that they had driven right by it for the second time. Still, neither one of them had noticed the place, up close. Jeannie felt her frustration growing.

"This was really annoying. It's not like I needed to find the house for any particular reason, but this had become a sort of puzzle that I needed to solve. So I made Todd pull over and park at the top of the hill, and we sat there and sort of mapped out the landmarks, so we would know exactly when we should look for this house."

Having done that, Todd and Jeannie began slowly to drive through the valley for the third time. While he watched the road, she ticked off each landmark they passed. Within a few minutes, Jeannie knew that they were about to see the house.

"I told Todd, 'Okay, it's around this corner, on the left.' And we rounded the corner, and it wasn't there. I couldn't believe it. And then Todd pulled over to the shoulder, and parked the car, and said, 'But look what is there.'"

What Todd pointed out to Jeannie was the weathered and crumbling foundation of an old farmhouse. The area that would once have been the yard had been completely overtaken by wild grass and trees, but the grey remains of the house could be seen. Suddenly, it was obvious why the freshly painted farmhouse could not be found.

"We're pretty sure it was a type of apparition," said Todd. "I've heard of haunted houses, but this was like a ghost house!" he laughed.

Jeannie added her own conclusion. "We do believe in these kinds of things, so it wasn't that hard to accept. Still, believing something in theory and having an actual experience are worlds apart."

Unfortunately, the couple's return route took them through a different part of the province, and they haven't yet had another opportunity to search for their ghost house in the hills. Both say that they someday plan to, though.

"Someday we will go back," said Todd, adding, "and when we do, we'll remember to have our camera ready."

The Wallace Street Spectre

In November 1926, the *Regina Leader-Post* ran an article about a very active haunted house in the city's east end. Families had been moving in and out of the Wallace Street abode in rapid succession, and each short-term tenant had a story to tell.

The first family interviewed was living in the house in 1924 when they met the ghost. The spirit took the form of a beautiful woman. In her hands she carried a bible with Romanian text on the cover. The family members, who had been mourning the loss of a relative in Romania, weren't sure how to interpret the vision—but they did know what to do about it. After three ghostly appearances, they packed up and moved away.

The next renters never saw the apparition, but heard noises that were unnerving and difficult to explain. The racket would begin with a thumping in the attic, followed immediately by similar noises in the cellar, and would conclude with the sharp, crashing sound of breaking glass. This happened every evening until, finally, after only four months in the house, the people found other accommodations.

The *Leader-Post* did not say whether the house stood vacant for a time, but it might have, for the next reported incident did not happen until nearly one year later. While a young mother sat nursing her baby in the kitchen of the house, she glanced up and saw the phantom of the beautiful lady with radiant, streaming hair. This time the ghost held no bible, but had her slender white hands joined in prayer. When the young mother made the sign of the cross, the ghost immediately turned and disappeared down the cellar stairs. Although the husband was described as "a robust specimen," he apparently did not feel fit enough to take on that which he did not understand. That night, a dray carried all of the couple's earthly possessions to a new address. They had lived in the Wallace Street house only one month.

By that time, the dwelling had gained a reputation in Regina. It was a matter of interest to both those who believed in ghosts and those who did not. While the house sat temporarily vacant, a well-known painter in the city thought he would take the opportunity to disprove all the "fanciful tales." Having clearly expressed that he had no fear of ghosts, the fellow and two friends visited the place late one evening. He had not even opened the door fully, however, before his courage was stripped away. An unearthly moan had sounded from within the house, and heavy, dragging footsteps could be heard coming toward the entranceway. The painter, quickly forgetting his public boasts, turned and fled. His friends, who had been waiting by the gate, were practically debilitated with laughter. When later asked by the *Leader-Post* what had become of the great ghost hunter, they snickered and replied, "He is running yet!"

During the week in which the newspaper story about the haunted house ran, it was said that "a rather well built car repair man... [had] taken up quarters there with a friend." Although he had spent only a few days in the place, the mechanic felt able to explain away all the ghost stories that had been told. With a confident air, he dismissed what the first family saw as "the reflection of a peculiarly formed chimney against the wall of the kitchen," or perhaps the shadows cast by clothing hung out on a line in a neighbour's yard. He attributed the attic noises to gusts of wind, which shook the tin plating, and the cellar noises to a cat. The man concluded by saying that he was not afraid to live in the house, did not believe in ghosts, and furthermore did not believe that ghosts had ever visited there.

Unfortunately, there is no way of knowing how long the man lived in that notorious house on Wallace Street, or if anything that happened there ever changed his strong, skeptical opinion.

A House Full of Spirits

There are a number of ghost stories associated with a large, older house that sits on Clifton Avenue in Moose Jaw. For nearly 30 years, residents of the haunted home have reported a variety of paranormal experiences. The following tales are those collected from just one family who lived there for a period of time.

The family's teenaged son had a friend sleeping over. The two boys were in a bedroom in the basement and on the verge of falling asleep, when one suddenly felt that someone was standing at the foot of the bed, watching them. As he opened his eyes, he felt a powerful rush of air move over him. He and his friend spoke at the same time:

"Hey, are you awake?"

"Did you just feel that!"

Both teens felt an immediate need to leave the basement. They spent the majority of the night sitting in the kitchen, drinking coffee and talking about the chilling experience that they had shared.

One of the house's resident spirits was seen by several members of the family. She is a little girl in a white nightgown. This quiet little spectre is never threatening, but likes simply to stand in one spot and watch those around her. When she has seen enough, her image fades away.

The father of the family, a no-nonsense type who is retired from the Armed Forces, witnessed a number of apparitions in his home. On one particularly unsettling occasion, the man awoke from a deep sleep to see two Doberman pinschers suspended in the air above his bed. The animals snarled and growled at him menacingly, then abruptly vanished.

Although the phantoms were seen throughout the house, the family suspected that they may have made the attic their home. Every night, the door leading to the attic was tightly closed. Often, in the morning, it was found wide open. Eventually, a padlock managed to keep the door securely shut. The ghosts still wandered about freely, though, and may still be doing so today.

THE
PARANORMAL
PAST

Ghost stories are a wonderfully entertaining way to learn about our past. Sometimes, they are bound to significant historical events. In other cases, they preserve the details of social history, through personal stories that accentuate the lifestyle, language, and customs of a certain time.

Each of the following stories features a sensational Saskatchewan ghost— and is seasoned with the flavour of a different era.

The Animal

It was nothing fancy, but it sure looked good. Eddie's mother had cut some big slices of fresh bread, slathered them with butter and made sandwiches with the ham left over from the previous night's supper. There were pickles and a few generous wedges of johnnycake with smears of honey. It all went into the battered aluminum pail that served as a picnic basket of sorts, and was handed over to the boy.

"Get this out to your father and the other men, now. They're sure to be hungry."

It was only mid-morning, but the crew had been in the field since dawn. Eddie knew from experience that they would be more than ready for a break and grateful for the food he was bringing. He liked his job of carrying out the snack. At seven years of age, he was a bit too young and a lot too small for the kind of heavy work that his father and the two hired hands did, but he was able to help in his own way, and that made him feel important.

Every morning at the same time, Eddie went out to the fields. Each time, he walked for some distance along the same path near the line of trees before setting out in the direction of that day's work site. He always strode along confidently, humming a tune. He would swing the pail first in one hand and then the other, savouring the satisfying weight of it. Eddie particularly enjoyed the walk because it gave him some time to anticipate the rewarding moment when he would hand the snack over to his father, who would always beam down at him and say, "Steady Eddie! What a good man to bring us some food!"

The day was warm but a little cloudy, and still, which made Eddie think there would be some rain before the sun set. The quiet was cut only by the sound of his own worn boots, tramping on the

A young boy in rural Saskatchewan encountered a terrifying paranormal creature while delivering lunch to the men in the field.

path. Once he was halfway down the line of trees, though, just out of sight of the house, there was another sound.

It was low and steady—so steady, in fact, that Eddie at first mistook it for the distant rumble of a train. When the noise grew closer and more intense, he knew he was wrong. It wasn't a rumble, it was a growl. There was an animal, somewhere in the trees, that was watching him.

Eddie felt a nervous sweat beginning to bead on his forehead. He kept walking, but veered away from the trees as far as he could. Every few seconds, he dared to glance back, hoping to see some movement that would tell him whether the animal was following him or laying in wait. He could see nothing. The menacing snarl became louder, but in the boy's frightened state, he found it impossible to pinpoint the source.

Eddie had been doing what he knew to be the right thing in such a situation. He had quickened his pace but continued to walk calmly and purposefully. He made no sudden or threatening movements, and he listened carefully for sounds that might tell him where the animal was. The growling had intensified, but as far as Eddie could tell, it was still coming from the trees. Then suddenly and without warning it was behind him. Eddie could hear the wet, salivating sound of the beast's jowls and feel its hot breath on his neck. It seemed too late to do the mature, safe, right thing, anymore. Eddie broke into a run.

He ran, and paid no attention to the vegetation that whipped his legs. He fell once, hard, but got up and going again without missing a beat. Eddie veered into the field and ran until his lungs felt like a pair of hot stones in his chest. He then realized two things at once: he couldn't take another step, and he couldn't hear the vicious, hungry growling anymore. The boy slowed to a stumbling walk, turned around to confirm that he was no longer being hunted, and collapsed in the midst of the wheat. Several minutes passed. Eddie's breathing calmed, and the chaotic black and white lights stopped blooming before his eyes. He wondered vaguely if he was very late, and if his father was worrying about him. And, on the heels of that thought, he remembered the food.

Somewhere along the line, Eddie had dropped, or thrown, the pail. That might have been the thing that saved him. Perhaps the animal had stopped chasing him to gobble the sliced ham. Still, he felt bad about having to go tell the work crew that there would be nothing to eat until lunch. Eddie was feeling less like a valuable member of the team as he headed off to deliver the bad news.

"Are you sayin' you run up against a bear, boy? 'Cause I ain't never heard of a bear coming this far out of the wilderness!" The older hired hand, a mostly toothless man named Gus, was having such a good laugh that he didn't seem to mind missing his meal. Even the tall, quiet fellow that had only been working for Eddie's father a month seemed to have an opinion.

"Sounds more like a wild dog, or the like," he said, "although, if you could feel it breathin' on your neck, that's a pretty tall order of a dog."

Eddie sat miserably on the ground and looked shyly up at his father, waiting for the viewpoint that counted most. The man looked concerned, but said little about Eddie's story. Instead, he turned to the hands. "Fellas, I'm sorry about the sandwiches," he said, "but if we just keep working now, this fence will be up before lunch time, and we can knock off a little early then." To his piti-ful-looking son, he added, "Eddie, you stay and lend a hand. We won't be long, and your mother won't mind." Eddie felt a great surge of relief. He couldn't bear the thought of walking back to the house by himself.

The hired hands worked together, putting posts into the ground. Eddie and his father followed behind, carefully unrolling the wire and nailing it on. It was really a one-man job, but Eddie's dad found ways for him to help. Every so often, when they were far enough behind that the other men couldn't hear, there would be a casual question.

"Do you think it was a wolf, Ed?" The boy shrugged. He really didn't know. "So you didn't get a proper look at it, then?" Eddie shook his head. "But you outran it?" Eddie began to chafe under the subtle interrogation.

"I think it stopped to eat up the food I dropped," he said, irri-tably. "Probably, that's all it wanted."

Eddie's dad nodded. "Could be. And that reminds me—you

and I better go back to the house the way you came. As long as we collect that pail, your mother won't ever have to know that her sandwiches were eaten up by some animal."

An hour later, Eddie's father called out to the hired men that they should pack it up. "Go straight on to the house," he instructed them. "Don't be saying anything to the missus about Eddie's wild animal. Just eat your lunch, and the boy and I will be along shortly." Eddie and his dad hammered wire onto the last of the posts, then started walking. They followed the path of trampled grain that Eddie had created as he ran frantically through the field. Neither of them spoke until they came to the line of trees.

"You tell me where you heard it," Eddie's father said.

"I don't know," the boy mumbled. "All along here." It was then he spotted the dull gleam of the aluminum pail in a patch of weeds. "There it is," Eddie pointed, feeling some small sense of accomplishment. The two walked over to fetch the bucket, which now featured a new dent. It lay on its side, with the carefully packed sandwiches spilled out all around it. Nothing had been touched.

"It looks like your animal wasn't hungry, Eddie." The boy's father picked up a sandwich that hadn't fallen out into the dirt, and took a bite. He then stood up straight and looked around thoughtfully. "You were running over here?" he asked, indicating the patch of scrubby ground close to the field. Eddie nodded. "And you say the thing was right behind you?" Again, the boy nodded. Eddie's father popped the last bite of bread and ham into his mouth and got down on his hands and knees. He examined the earth carefully, then got up and dusted off his knees. "All I can see is your tracks, Eddie. To be honest, I think you were just being chased by your imagination there this morning." The man chuckled and patted his son's shoulder with his weathered hand. "We've got our pail, let's get on home, now," he said.

Eddie felt a storm of conflicting emotions rising within him. He was grateful and relieved that his father wasn't angry, despite what he thought. But he knew that what had happened was real, and he was desperate for his dad to believe that. As the boy walked along beside his father, feeling wretched and trying to think of a solution, there began a distant, menacing sound.

"What's that?" cried Eddie. He grabbed his father's sleeve and yanked him to a stop. "Dad, what's that?"

Eddie's father listened to the low growling for a few seconds. His face was furrowed in concentration. "I don't know," he finally admitted. "A noise from up on the highway, maybe."

"Then why is it getting closer?" Eddie asked. It was true: the sound was nearer, and louder, and more feral than it had been only moments earlier. For the second time that day, the boy felt fear prickling his skin. When the growl turned into the snarling, jaw-snapping sounds that had been at his back only hours earlier, Eddie clutched his father's hand for reassurance. When he looked up into the man's face, however, his small sense of safety melted away. Eddie could see that his dad was scared, too. As scared as he was.

"Eddie, we have to walk. But calmly, very calmly," the man said. His steady voice was betrayed by his ashen face. As the two started along the path to the house, Eddie's father said one more thing. It frightened the boy more than anything else had that day. "If I tell you to run, you run," he said, quietly and firmly. "Go like hell for the house, and don't look back." All around them, the hidden creature made its threatening sounds, and Eddie thought he might cry. Instead, he walked and waited for what he knew was about to happen.

Seconds later, it did happen. The snarling that had been coming from everywhere was now coming from directly behind Eddie and his father. The boy could feel hot, stinking, animal breath on his back; he felt his scalp bristle. His dad must have felt it too, for all at once, he spun around to face the thing that was hunting them. His eyes widened in terror, and he screamed out a single word.

"Run!"

Eddie ran. He ran, and he began to sob, trying to close out the sounds of the vicious attack that was taking place behind him. He knew that the animal wasn't chasing him and that he could make it safely to the house, but the knowledge did nothing to ease his fear. Without his father, nothing would ever really be safe again. That thought seemed to slap the tears off his cheeks, and Eddie stopped in his tracks. He turned. And despite what he saw, he began to run back.

Eddie's father was pinned to the ground, trying in vain to protect his face with his arms. Weighing him down was a shape—that was the only way to describe it—a shape that was as misty and insubstantial as steam from the kettle in some spots, and as solid as rock in others. The composition of the thing kept shifting, so that one moment, Eddie would see a definite tail thrashing from the effort of the fight, and the next, a snapping jaw lined with razor teeth. Eddie didn't give his mind time to comprehend the horror, and he didn't know what he was going to do. He just ran to his dad. When he was close enough to smell the tangy combination of animal sweat and blood, he screamed out.

"Get away from my dad! Get away!"

"Eddie!" The boy's father twisted to one side and looked at his son with terrified eyes. "Go to the house! The *house!*" A solid animal paw appeared out of the twisting vapour and batted the man's head to the other side. Eddie saw a pinkish spray fly up into the air. He thought that he was going to be sick, and then he stopped thinking at all, and acted.

The handle of the battered aluminum pail was still clutched in Eddie's small hand. With one great motion that nearly dislocated his shoulder, the boy wound up and sent the pail flying. It twisted and sailed through the air as Eddie stumbled and fell flat to the ground with the effort. He looked up just in time to see that his aim had been beautiful.

The lunch pail cut a path through the shape that hovered above Eddie's father. The ferocious sound that the wild thing had been making stopped suddenly. Filling the vacancy of sound came a high-pitched yelp and a pained whining. Eddie got up on his knees and clawed the ground, looking for another missile. He found a hard clump of earth and threw it into the air directly over his father. Again, there was the high whistling cry of an animal in pain.

"I said get!" Eddie's voice was louder now, and more confident. He was on his feet again, and had his hand curled around a smooth, hefty stone. When he sent it slicing through the mist, he felt the muscle in his biceps burning. "Get away!" he yelled, and reached for a heavy piece of broken branch. It was a weapon he would not need. The writhing animal shape was leaving. Unsteadily, it rolled off Eddie's father and began to slink toward the safety of the line of trees. As it moved, it became wispy and vague. Then the thing vanished with a barely audible whimper.

For a long time, Eddie stared at the place where the beast had become nothing. The air was still, the field was quiet, and the boy suddenly felt very tired. He wished he was sitting in a chair by the stove, or tucked comfortably into the quilts of his own bed. He wanted to be at home, and it took his father's voice to remind him why he had come back at all.

"Eddie? Are you all right, son?"

Eddie jumped. For a few seconds he had actually forgotten that his dad lay on the ground behind him. Slowly, the boy turned, preparing himself to face the worst. He had seen brief flashes of the phantom animal's teeth and claws, he had seen the bright spray of blood in the air, and he knew his father must be badly hurt. But Eddie could not prepare himself for what he was about to see.

His father was sitting up. He looked shaken, he looked shocked, but he was whole and unmarked. With a grunt, he pushed himself to his feet. "Eddie, you okay to walk?" he asked. "'Cause if it's all the same to you, I'd like to get the hell away from here." Eddie nodded, and the two started off toward the house.

"Dad, you're not even scratched," Eddie said. The man nodded. "And where you got attacked—there's no mark on the ground. There are no tracks!" The boy could not believe that there was no evidence of all he had seen. His father stopped, turned to Eddie, and placed both his large hands on the boy's slight shoulders.

"I know," he said. "And there's no sign that you saved my life, either. But you did."

Eddie didn't know how to respond, so he simply said, "We should get the lunch pail."

"Leave it," replied his father. They walked in silence the rest of the way, and it would be a long time before they spoke of the incident again.

After that, Eddie's father and the hired hands took lunch with them whenever they went out to the fields. It had to be things that wouldn't spoil in the sun, and Eddie's mother complained that the food would never taste as good. She couldn't understand why Eddie couldn't take the meal out as he always had. "That's a child's job," the father said. "Eddie's a man."

Eddie looked at his dad's face, and saw nothing but sincerity. For the rest of his life, he knew it to be true: he had grown up overnight, by passing the strangest of supernatural tests on a southern Saskatchewan farm.

The Lafleche Cemetery Wraith

One March evening in 1936, two men were walking along a road that led northeast of Lafleche. The friends were more than familiar with the route, for one of them lived in town, and the other on a farm a short distance away. Whenever they socialized together, it was customary for one to walk the other at least part of the way home. At the Lafleche Cemetery, which was about a mile and a half outside of town, they usually parted ways.

On this particular evening, the soothing balm of spring was in the air, and the men lingered a while before saying goodbye. They leaned casually against the cemetery fence, smoking and exchanging yarns, until something strange caught their attention.

In the centre of the graveyard, the friends saw a human figure moving to and fro in a slow and even manner. The apparition was blurred around the edges and seemed not to notice them as they gaped at it. Determined to find out if their imagination was playing tricks on them, they hopped the fence and went to investigate. When they reached the spot, however, no trace of it could be found. Perplexed, the friends returned to the fence. Once there, they saw the mysterious shape moving again.

By this time, both young men were convinced that there was something very strange happening in the cemetery. They thought it best to stick together and go back into town. There, they related their experience to several people. A subsequent report in the *Regina Leader-Post* offered proof of their sincerity, saying that "to show their bona fides, [the men] offered to take affidavits as to the truth of their statements."

A Ghost Affects the Vote

On April 27, 1942, the *Regina Leader-Post* ran an interesting item that had come from its Yorkton Bureau. According to the article, a plebiscite was to be held at Poplar Springs School, north of Yorkton, on that day. It was suggested that the outcome of the vote had perhaps already been affected by one of the area's earliest settlers—a man who had been dead for many decades.

On the Thursday prior to the vote, speeches were to be held at Poplar Springs School. Dr. C.J. Houston and Steve Penarowski were two of the speakers scheduled for that day. Only a hundred yards into their four-mile journey to Poplar Springs, however, the vehicle that the men were driving became stuck in the mud. It took 15 men to push the car from its mucky trap, and one of them pointed out to the two travellers that, following a recent rain, the entire road was likely to be as soft and treacherous. Dr. Houston and Mr. Penarowski decided that it would be wise to take another road to their destination.

It just so happened that the speakers' alternate route took them directly over the grave of one of southeast Saskatchewan's pioneers. The rural burial site had been reported to be haunted since the day someone saw fit to build a road squarely over top of it. Usually around midnight, local farmers often saw a phantom light hovering over the exact spot where the settler had been laid to rest. It seemed obvious that the man's spirit was unhappy about the disturbance of his grave. According to the *Leader-Post* article, he may also have had an opinion to express in the impending plebiscite.

As Houston and Penarowski drove unwittingly over the haunted spot, the road suddenly collapsed under their vehicle's wheels. In a matter of seconds, the car became hopelessly trapped, with two wheels resting in the settler's grave.

The two would-be speakers were terribly discouraged, but not yet beaten. They first tried to jack the car out of the hole. When that failed, they trudged to a nearby farm and enlisted the help of a man and his team of horses. The farmer was quite willing to lend a hand, but though the horses sweated and strained, the mired car would not budge. Eventually, the doubletree to which the horses were harnessed snapped, and the three men were forced to admit defeat.

Luckily, another local resident happened by at that moment. This man was driving a powerful five-horse team, and offered his assistance. It was gratefully accepted.

Midnight approached as the larger team of horses was hitched to the vehicle. Several neighbours began appearing on the scene—not to help, for they hadn't known anything was amiss, but to encounter the ghost. The people had noticed the lantern lights bobbing around the grave after dark and thought that the spirit was having a wild night. They were disappointed to discover that the pioneer's spectre had not materialized, but interested to note that he had managed to trap a car.

With five brawny horses pulling diligently at the vehicle, it was finally freed from its awkward predicament. The *Leader-Post* summed up the aftermath:

Dr. Houston and Mr. Penarowski paid the farmers $4 for getting the car out of the grave and wondered whether Prime Minister Mackenzie King would see that their dry cleaning bill, a considerable item, was paid. Dr. Houston lost his rubbers many times and found them again, but finally failed to recover them, which, in view of the rubber shortage, added to his difficulties.

The greatest loss for the two men was that they missed their opportunity to speak before the plebiscite. They counted themselves lucky, however, that although they passed midnight in the grave of the old pioneer, they did not encounter his eerie apparition.

Dandelions for Margaret

For the children who grew up in rural Saskatchewan in the lean Depression years, there were not many ready-made amusements.

"We didn't have rooms full of toys and video games," recalled a woman named Margaret, who spent her youth on a farm near Saskatoon. "You counted yourself lucky if your family had a radio. We used to make our own fun, and we turned whatever was around us into a playground."

One rather odd choice of a playground was an old country cemetery not far from the small school house that Margaret attended. Many of the children enjoyed spending time there, playing, talking and making up stories about the people whose names appeared on the headstones.

"We were never disrespectful," stressed Margaret. "If anything, we had great respect for the people buried there. At least we came to visit them! Not many others did. It was just a sort of private place for us... the only grownups who were there couldn't boss us around."

In an overgrown and forgotten country cemetery, a young girl received a supernatural gift of gratitude.

During the school year, Margaret would visit the cemetery with her friends. During the summer months, however, she frequently went alone. It was then that she spent more time examining each marker in the tiny, ragged burial ground, and imagining how each of those lives must have been lived. One grave in particular really captured her imagination.

"There was one tombstone I would always visit. It was a woman's grave, and her name was Margaret, like mine. She had died very young, just after World War I, so it might have been the Spanish Flu, or something. Anyway, I just made a point of always visiting her. I'd talk to her a little and tell her things, and usually I'd leave her a bouquet of 'flowers.'"

Margaret laughed when she recalled this, for her floral bouquet was normally made up of dandelions. It wasn't that there were no wild flowers to be found during the prairie summer, but rather that 10-year-old Margaret simply thought that dandelions, with their brilliant yellow blooms, were the most beautiful

blossoms to be found. She seldom left the cemetery without plac-
ing a sunny bundle of them on the late Margaret's grave.

As the years passed and the little girl grew into a teenager, she
spent less and less time climbing over the weathered wooden fence
that surrounded the graveyard. There were other things to think
about, such as friends, and boys, and the community hall dances
that she was sometimes permitted to attend with her parents. One
day when she was 14, Margaret realized that she hadn't been by the
cemetery in nearly a year.

"I just kind of felt an urge to visit," she said. "And since I was
going to go away to school soon, I thought it might be nice to say
goodbye."

It was a beautiful June day. Margaret dutifully finished her chores
at home, then strolled down the dusty road for a mile to the cemetery. Along the way, she gathered up a bouquet of dandelions to
leave at the other Margaret's grave. "By then, I knew that was kind
of stupid," she said, "but it was a tradition, so I stuck with it."

Margaret was feeling far too mature to hop the fence, so she
unlatched and carefully pushed at the ancient gate. The posts
had settled so far into the ground that she couldn't make it swing
more than two feet, but it was enough to allow her to slip
through. Once inside, she walked over to the grave site she had
so often visited, and sat down cross-legged on the grassy earth.
The canopy of poplar leaves created little dancing spots of sun
and shadow on the weather-worn headstone. Margaret brushed
a few twigs away from her namesake's eternal resting place and
soaked in the peaceful atmosphere of the forgotten little piece
of land. A bird chirped happily in a nearby tree, and insects
hummed lazily through the warm, summer air. Margaret drew
a deep, contented breath. Then she spent a few minutes talking
to the late Margaret, telling her about all the exciting changes in
her life. When she finished speaking, she remembered the little

bunch of dandelions, already becoming limp on the ground beside her.

"I picked them up and sort of arranged them nicely, and then said, 'Here you go, Margaret. These will have to last you for a while,'" Margaret recalled. She then set the blossoms down at the base of the headstone, and proceeded to have one of the most affecting experiences of her life.

"I didn't know how to describe it then," she said, "but now I guess I would say that the atmosphere changed. Everything in that cemetery was the same: I could hear the birds, and the flies buzzing, and I could see the sun, and the grass, and the breeze moving the leaves. But it was like I was inside a glass bubble. The air right around me was different. I was sort of detached. And then—I'll never forget it—I felt this pressure on my shoulder, as though someone had placed a cool hand there, and I heard the words 'thank you.' It wasn't out loud, it was like someone whispered it inside my head. And a split second later, everything was back to normal."

Normal, except that Margaret had experienced something that was magnificent and rare. More than 60 years later, she still treasures the memory of that moment, when she received the gift of gratitude from beyond the grave.

The Porcupine River Wraith

The men were sitting in a semicircle, a collection of bright plaid flannel shirts in stark contrast to the muted autumn colours of the forest. They nudged the wet, brown leaves with their boots, and occasionally someone would clear his throat. Aside from that, they waited silently. Every twig that was rustled by a small, scurrying animal grabbed their attention. Every birdcall was noted. The reassuring, returning footsteps of their leader could not be heard, however, and despite the powerful rifles that rested in their hands, the men looked nervous.

Claude Arteaux was more nervous than the rest. It was his father who was leading the group of hunters, and fully 20 minutes had passed since he had ventured down to the river to investigate a noise. Actually, it was not just a noise. Noises were routine in the northern woods, which teemed with life. This had been a bone-chilling shriek, an unearthly sound not belonging to or expected in the clean wilderness of northern Saskatchewan.

It had been too long. Claude stood and cocked his rifle. "I'd best go take a look," he told the other men, and headed off to follow his father's trail through the brush. It was the fall of 1939, and the young hunting and fishing guide was about to see something that would change his belief system forever.

Claude cautiously made his way down to the bank of the Porcupine River. He then crept northward, keeping his rifle ready and his eyes alert every step of the way. His ears were filled with the peaceful sounds of rushing water, but his mind seemed intent upon replaying the horrid sound he had heard only an hour earlier. The anguished shriek had paled the most seasoned members of the hunting party, including Claude's unshakable father. "That's no animal," he had said, before leaving to investigate. In such a remote place, that which wasn't an animal or a hunter was a cause for concern.

When Claude had made his way a quarter-mile up the river, he saw his father. The man was standing on the bank, staring out over the churning water. He appeared transfixed by something, and the relief Claude felt at seeing him was quickly replaced with unease when he saw what his father was staring at. There, hovering like a mist over the river, was an eerie, phantom-like shape. The form writhed and pulsed. Claude's father stood with his arms hanging limply by his sides. His rifle lay forgotten on the ground. He seemed unable to look away.

"Dad! *Dad*!" Claude shouted over the sounds of the river. This seemed to break the spell, and the elder Arteaux spun around and raised a warning hand.

"Don't come any closer!" he begged his son. "Turn your back and don't look around!"

Claude was frightened, but followed his father's directions without question. For several minutes he stood that way, hardly daring to breathe. Finally, his father was by his side. In a shaking voice, the older man said, "Let's get out of here right away. I've just seen the lost river wraith, and you know what that means!"

Claude stared at his father in shock. "Sure I know what that's supposed to mean, but it's a silly legend, isn't it?" He could see the answer in his dad's ashen face.

"It's more than a legend," the man said, flatly. "I just saw the thing with my own eyes."

The story was local lore, known to anyone who had grown up, as Claude had, in the small town of Stony Rapids. As people sat around their campfires during the brief summer, they loved to tell the gruesome tale of a haunted spot on the Porcupine River, no more than 50 miles away. While the firelight danced on their faces, they would explain that there had been a murderer who was shot along the riverbank by a vengeful vigilante mob. But he did not die from the bullets, the storytellers would say—that would have been too swift and kind. The mob who had gunned him down saw fit to drag the man into the river and pin his legs beneath a heavy boulder. There they left him to die of his wounds. Ever since, it was said that the spirit of the dead man haunted that spot on the river. The spectre was destined to remain there for all eternity, and any mortal who was luckless enough to see it was doomed to die within a year.

Claude knew the legend well, and now he knew that there really was a ghost to be seen at that spot on the Porcupine River. But the curse? He couldn't allow himself to believe it. Especially regarding his father, who was hale and hearty, and only 52 years of age.

Three months later, Claude believed in the curse, too. His robust father lay on his deathbed, offering a few final words of advice to his son.

"You know where the wraith is," he gasped. "Don't ever go near that place on the river again." Claude promised as his father died.

Claude Arteaux carried on his father's work as a hunting and fishing guide, and always conscientiously avoided the cursed stretch of river. A friend of Claude's, a man named Roger Leclaire, made frequent jokes about his "silly superstition."

"One day I will go looking for your 'river wraith,'" he laughed. "I am brave enough to stare into the face of a little harmless water spray!" True to his word, Roger Leclaire did travel to the haunted spot on the river that Claude had told him about. And he must have looked into what he thought to be nothing more than mist rising from the churning water. There was no way to know for certain, however, because the man's lifeless body was later pulled from the Porcupine River. His face, it was said, was contorted in an expression of sheer terror.

The townspeople of Stony Rapids wondered what had killed Roger Leclaire, but Claude Arteaux knew. Roger's death had been further proof, although Claude hadn't needed any, that the lost wraith of the Porcupine River was much more than just a legend.

Claude went on to spend decades working as a wilderness guide in the area. He knew the best areas to hunt, and places along the river where the water teemed with fish. Despite occasional requests, however, he never once took anyone close to the haunted spot on the Porcupine River. After all, a good hunter always knows when he has become the prey, and his weapon has become useless. Two deaths had been more than enough to convince Claude Arteaux that the famous Porcupine River wraith was deadly and real.

A Ghost With Good Timing

"In 1943, I was working in a little lunch-counter type of restaurant in Prince Albert," recalled a woman named Dorothy. "It was just a greasy spoon, but the tips could be pretty good." The place had a few narrow booths along one wall, but was dominated mainly by a big horseshoe-shaped counter. During the busy breakfast and lunch rushes, Dorothy and another waitress both worked inside the horseshoe, taking orders, filling coffee cups, and serving up plates of hot specials. Few of their customers chose to sit in a booth, for chatting and joking with the two women was considered part of the restaurant's appeal.

"I had a whole lot of fun working there," Dorothy remembered. "Everyone got along, we had some good regulars and everyone liked a joke. Having a good sense of humour can help you get by, too. Like whenever I'd make a mistake, or the other girl would, we'd look dead serious and blame it on 'the ghost.' That was such a long-running gag that some customers would come in and say, 'Dorothy, I'll have a bowl of soup and a fried-egg sandwich, and don't let the ghost get near it.'"

One afternoon, the ghost jokes were overheard by a new customer. The man lingered, drinking coffee, long after most of the lunch customers had left. When Dorothy came over to refill his cup for the fourth time, he made her an offer.

"I know an empty house where there's a real ghost," he said. "I've seen it many times. I could take you there some night, if you like."

Dorothy was intrigued, and made a date to meet the stranger outside the restaurant that evening. Years later, she would shake her head at such foolish behaviour. "A lot of us girls were pretty naive, then. But he was an older, nicely dressed man—and honestly, I didn't think of it as a date. I guess he did, though."

It was August, so there were still hours of daylight remaining when the man pulled up to the curb in front of the restaurant in his late-model sedan. Dorothy climbed into the passenger seat and was a little surprised when the man leaned over and kissed her. "The ghost won't come out until after dark," he said, as he put the car in gear. "So let's get a couple of drinks." Dorothy wanted to seem calm and worldly, so she agreed. Ten minutes later, she was sitting in a bar with a powerful, foul-tasting highball in front of her.

"I was used to drinking the odd beer," Dorothy said, "and I'd had my dad's homemade wine, but this was hard liquor. It tasted awful."

Despite her distaste for the drink, Dorothy's date was insistent that she keep up with him. Each time he ordered a drink for himself, he ordered one for Dorothy, too. Fortunately, a sympathetic bartender interceded silently on the young woman's behalf. "When I took the first sip of my second drink," Dorothy remembered, "it was nothing more than ginger ale. I had no problem matching that fellow glass for glass, then."

The evening wore on and Dorothy grew more bored. Eventually she stood up, grabbed her purse and made an excuse about having to be up early the next morning. "No, no—wait," her date slurred. "We haven't seen the ghost yet." The man threw some money on the bar and took Dorothy's arm. As they walked out to the parking lot, she noticed that it had become very dark while they had been inside. Even the stars and moon were hidden by an overcast sky.

"It's not far from here, this haunted house," the man said as he started the car. In the reflected glow of the headlights, Dorothy thought she saw an odd, humourless smile touch the man's lips. Suddenly she wished she was back in the bar with the understanding bartender. Even more than that, she wished she was in her cheap, rented room above the restaurant, curled up in bed with a paperback romance. Mostly she wished she had had enough sense to say "no" to this stranger, hours earlier. But the car was moving, and the lights of Prince Albert were fading as the man drove her out of town.

After a few miles, the man turned onto a secondary road, then down a long, gravel drive that was obscured with shaggy pine trees. The drive led to a hidden yard with a two-storey house that sat as dark as a tomb.

"I remember that man leaning over after he stopped the car, and he looked just like the cat that ate the canary," said Dorothy. "He said, 'We're here. Are you scared, yet?' I can tell you that by that point I was, but I wasn't thinking much about the ghost."

The man led Dorothy across the overgrown yard to the rotting front porch. In the dark, he showed her where she could step without breaking through the disintegrating planks. Using a small piece of heavy wire, he easily picked the lock. The door swung open with a rusty groan of its hinges, and the couple walked inside.

There was a coal-oil lamp sitting on the cold, unused iron surface of the stove. The man struck a wooden match against the stove top, and touched the blooming yellow flame to the lamp's wick. As flickering, dim light washed across the kitchen and living room, Dorothy could see that the place had been deserted for some time. Thick dust had settled softly on every surface. Spiders had constructed elaborate webs on the few pieces of broken furniture that remained. Dorothy asked the man how he knew about this house, and he gave her a vague answer. She asked him how often he visited it, and he was even more evasive. Dorothy could see one place where there were fresh footprints in the dust, however—on the stairs that led to the second floor bedrooms. She would later remember the moment well.

"I was just thinking about this, and it was like he was reading my mind, because this fellow suddenly said, 'Oh, we have to go upstairs. That's where the ghost is.' I was going to say "no," but then I thought, what difference does it make? I was already stuck there. I was already in trouble. So I went up the stairs."

At the top of the staircase, the man pointed to the doorway at the end of the hall. "The ghost shows up in there," he said. "There's a mattress on the floor, so we can be comfortable while we wait." As he started toward the bedroom, however, Dorothy paused. She could see a cracked mirror and basin in the small room to her right.

"Give me a minute," she said. "I want to use the bathroom." The man looked back at her impatiently.

"There's no water," he said.

"I know," Dorothy hesitated, then improvised. "I want to fix my hair and lipstick. Can I have the lamp?" The man looked amused, but handed over the lantern. He walked into the bedroom, and Dorothy stepped into the tiny washroom, having bought herself precious seconds to formulate a plan.

Dorothy's mind raced over her options. It was too far back to town to consider walking. The man had his car keys in the pocket of his trousers, so it wouldn't be easy to get them. There was no way she could overpower him, and there was no one nearby who might help her. Dorothy gazed into the speckled mirror with its jagged fracture. Her face was split into two mismatched halves, and each one wore a look of fright. Apparently she was not alone, however, for at that moment, a scream pierced the air.

Startled, Dorothy ran out of the bathroom to the end of the short hallway. She very nearly collided with her date, who came stumbling out of the bedroom, clutching his shoes and his jacket near his chest. "Run!" he gasped, "Run! There really *is* a goddamn ghost!" With that, he tore down the hall and half-stumbled, half-slid down the narrow wooden stairs. Dorothy was too shocked to follow, however, and stood staring into the dark bedroom. Then, in a split second, she realized that her real problem had very likely been averted. Relief washed over her, and she experienced a little boost of courage.

"I was standing there, and I thought, if you were stupid enough to get into this situation, at least be brave enough to see what you came for," said Dorothy. In three bold steps, she was inside the bedroom.

"At first, I couldn't see a thing," she recalled, "because I'd left the lamp down the hall, remember. But then I heard something, like a shooshing sound, and I could feel the air swirling around me. It was cold, but I knew there was nothing to be afraid of. When that pocket of air swirled away from me into the corner, I could see that it had a little light of its own. Sort of a hazy glow." Dorothy then realized that, if she didn't want to be stranded, she had better leave. She turned and walked out the bedroom door, but not before speaking to the faint, white mist in the corner. "I told it, 'thank you'" she said.

Outside, Dorothy found her date depositing the remainder of his cocktails in a stinking puddle between his feet. She climbed into the car and waited patiently until the man was steady enough to get behind the wheel. The two then shared a silent ride back into Prince Albert.

As the man pulled into the curb beside the restaurant, Dorothy's curiosity overcame her. "I asked him what he had seen up there," she remembered. The man's answer wasn't entirely satisfying. "He told me, 'I don't know, but I don't ever want to see it again!'" she laughed. As she stood on the sidewalk and watched the sedan drive off into the distance, Dorothy was certain of two things: the man was unlikely ever to lure another girl out to the deserted farmhouse, and she would never again fall for such a ruse. One other small thing changed, as well.

"I didn't joke so much about our 'ghost' at the restaurant, after that," Dorothy admitted. "I just had more respect for spirits and things, and I felt that I shouldn't even pretend to be using one as a scapegoat."

Dorothy never met another ghost, but always remained grateful to the one that rescued her in a dusty, deserted Saskatchewan farmhouse.

The Haunted Hen House

In 1963, Iris Couster, from Craven, Saskatchewan, wrote about an unexplained incident which had taken place more than a half-century before.

The year was 1907, and Iris was a child, living with her younger brother and parents on an isolated homestead. One day in early June, the children were looking out the window of the family's two-room log shack. They watched with great interest as a tall man in a black felt hat emerged from a stand of trees near the house. Iris and her brother called their mother over, and all three stared at the stranger as he passed no more than 15 feet in front of the window, then proceeded down the path toward the half-open door of the hen house. The man disappeared into the little building, leaving his small audience confused.

"In those days homesteads were lonely places," wrote Iris, so the three waited anxiously for their visitor to reemerge. After ten minutes, however, they began to doubt that he would. Iris's mother, who had become concerned, awakened her husband from his nap. He went to investigate, but found no one keeping the chickens company. It was extremely strange, Iris recalled, because "there was only one door to the hen house, and if the man came out we would have seen him." And there was another mystery to contemplate: although it had been raining for several days, the stranger in the black hat had left no tracks in the soft mud. Iris's father accused his family of letting their imagination get the better of them, and the matter was dropped. That is, until one month later.

In the early evening of a hot day in July, Iris and her mother were standing in the open doorway of their home. Suddenly the dog began to bark excitedly, drawing their attention to the nearby grove of trees. There, once more, was the tall stranger. Again, he walked out of the brush and passed within yards of the house. Again, he proceeded down the dirt path toward the hen house, into which he vanished. This time, however, his appearance caused more fear, because Iris's father was away and her brother had gone down to the end of the field to fetch the cow. The boy would have to pass by the side of the hen house when he returned. Nervously, Iris and her mother watched to see if the man would come out, but there was no sign of him. As they waited, Iris's brother came bounding up the path, chasing the cow. Before they could call out a warning, he ducked into the hen house, where the animal's watering pail was kept. Within seconds, he appeared with the pail, looking quite unconcerned. "When we questioned him," said Iris, "he was surprised, as he had seen no one."

The spectre appeared one more time that summer. In late August, a distant neighbour was visiting Iris's mother for an afternoon. The conversation was interrupted when, once more, the dog began to yelp excitedly while staring at the trees. The same tall man in a black felt hat appeared, walked directly in front of the house, then headed down the path and turned into the hen house.

*Prairie farmyards are usually cluttered with a variety of outbuildings—
structures which are, apparently, not immune to hauntings.*

This time, the group summoned the courage to follow the phantom immediately, but were disappointed to find the little building
as empty as ever.

Iris later wrote:

> If it had been one person who had seen it, we
> could have put it down to an hallucination, but the first
> time there were three of us, the second time two of us,
> [and] the fourth time four of us, one being an outsider.

Iris recalled that, for many years, her mother enjoyed telling the
story. Each person who heard the tale offered a theory, but no one
could truly explain the presence of the mysterious spirit who
chose to haunt a hen house on a remote prairie homestead.

The Whispering Woman

"There were a lot of things that I didn't like about being the younger sister," a woman named Dolores once said of her childhood in Depression-era Saskatoon. "Mary would get to have things new, and by the time they were passed to me, they'd be threadbare and used up. And she was the first to do everything. She went to school first, she wore lipstick first, she even married before I did." There was one special experience that belonged solely to Dolores, however. It began when she was only twelve years old.

The two sisters shared a double bed in a small, upstairs room. This, too, was a vexation to Dolores, a light sleeper who was often awakened by Mary's tossing and snoring. One particular night, after counting every spidery crack in the bedroom's plaster ceiling, Dolores was finally drifting off to sleep. Suddenly she was pulled back to consciousness by a strange whispering sound. If Mary's begun talking in her sleep, thought the exhausted girl, then I'm going downstairs to spend the night in a chair. But when she opened her eyes, Dolores saw that her sister was resting quietly for a change, and that someone else was in the room.

"She was very, very beautiful," Dolores recalled, decades after the incident took place. The woman standing by the girls' bed had flowing, dark hair and a dusky complexion. She appeared to be Native, and wore an exquisitely beaded sheath made of supple-looking buckskin. Her shining eyes were nearly black in colour, and were fixed on Dolores's face. As the little girl stared at the apparition in amazement, the Native woman began to move her lips. She seemed to be speaking to Dolores, but all that came out was an incomprehensible whisper.

"It was like the wind was carrying her words away. That's the best I can describe it," Dolores later explained.

The young girl felt no fear, for the radiant spirit clearly meant no harm. For several minutes, they regarded each other; then the woman simply faded from sight. Dolores was left feeling calm and relaxed, and soon fell into a peaceful slumber.

For days, Dolores told no one about her incredible experience. "I never, ever told my parents," she said. "I knew how foolish that would have been." Eventually, however, she felt the need to share the story with someone and chose to talk to Mary.

Mary, a 15-year-old who considered herself quite worldly and knowledgeable, was three years older than her sister. As Dolores told her tale in descriptive detail, she was met with a cynical laugh. "Mary said I was a baby having silly dreams, and not to bother her. I decided right then and there that I would never tell her another secret, if I lived to be 100."

Months passed, and Dolores was pleased that the lovely raven-haired woman returned to visit on several occasions. Her appearance was always accompanied by the soothing whispering sounds and an atmosphere of calm that would lull the girl to sleep. What also pleased Dolores immensely was the fact that the woman seemed so completely focused upon her. Although Mary snored away conspicuously in the same bed, the ghost never spared the older girl a look.

"I saw her maybe five or six times, over a period of two years," explained Dolores. "Then an interesting thing happened, the summer I turned 14."

The "interesting thing" was a horrible case of influenza that kept Dolores bed-ridden for nearly six days. Since Mary had already had the bug and there were no spare beds, the girls continued to sleep together. Toward the end of her illness, when Dolores's fever finally broke, she fell into an extremely deep sleep. The familiar whispering sounds were not enough to rouse her. Mary, however, who had been complaining that her sister's feverish thrashing was preventing her beauty sleep, was more easily wakened. The next morning, as Dolores enjoyed her first full breakfast in a week, she noticed that her older sister kept looking at her strangely.

"It was days before she said anything," Dolores recalled. "But eventually, she couldn't keep it in. Mary knew that I was the only person she could tell her story to. Anyone else would think she was crazy."

What Mary finally told Dolores was that on that night, she woke up to the strange sound of someone whispering. She opened her eyes and was shocked to see the dark-haired woman that Dolores had once spoken of, standing beside the bed. The spirit was looking intently at Dolores, smiling encouragingly and whispering words that Mary could not properly hear or understand. The older girl must have cried out in fear, for the woman suddenly turned to meet her gaze. "Mary said that she didn't look happy to see her. Not happy at all," chuckled Dolores. It must have been true, for as soon as the lovely ghost saw Mary, her benevolent expression changed, and she quickly vanished from sight.

"Mary acted a little different after that night," Dolores later said. "She treated me with just a little more respect." As for the spirit, Dolores saw her several more times during her teen years. She never understood what the beautiful apparition was saying, but always enjoyed her visits—and always felt special to have been chosen for those moments.

Inspector Denny's Strange Case

Opinion seems to be divided on whether the events of this story, set in the Cypress Hills, took place in Saskatchewan or Alberta. Since it happened 30 years before the two provinces were even created and is a fascinating tale, I will take the liberty of including it here.

* * *

Inspector Cecil Edward Denny was one of the original officers of the North-West Mounted Police. He was stationed at Fort Walsh in the 1870s, a time when the Canadian West was very young and very wild. Denny was adept at handling volatile situations and dangerous people, and collected a wealth of exciting personal stories which he eventually, in retirement, parlayed into a writing career. The strangest of all his experiences demanded an entire book to itself, entitled *Riders of the Plains*. In it, Denny described an inexplicable event that took place in 1875.

Denny had decided one day to go on a hunting and fishing expedition. An experienced frontiersman, he loaded every necessity for the trip onto a packhorse. His plan was to travel overland to his destination accompanied by a Native guide. On the return trip, the guide would take the horse and supplies back along the same route, while Denny used a raft and enjoyed a scenic and exciting river voyage.

During his return by raft, the Inspector was overtaken by the wildest of rainstorms. Though it was the middle of a summer afternoon, the sky grew as black as night. Blinding sheets of rain poured down, furious winds and violently churning water whipped the raft uncontrollably, and thunder and lightening split the heavens. Denny knew that in order to survive the storm, he would have to sit it out. He beached his raft and found what little shelter he could.

There was a brief lull in the storm, during which Denny heard the nearby pounding of drums and familiar, rhythmic Native chanting. He was extremely relieved: surely the Natives would offer him some food and shelter, and help him dry his soaked clothing. Denny followed the sound to its source, a small encampment in a nearby clearing.

When the officer was close enough to identify the artistic designs that decorated the teepees, he grew even more pleased. It was a Cree camp that he was approaching—good news, since the Crees were helpful friends of the North-West Mounted Police. However, as Denny staggered toward the clearing through the final few hundred yards of heavy, rain-soaked brush, he began to notice something strange.

The Natives moved easily about the camp, seemingly oblivious to the storm. Naked children played together happily, and women sat at the open doors of their tents preparing food. The men wandered about the camp, inappropriately dressed against the torrential rain and seeming not to care. There were even a few shaggy horses grazing as contentedly as if it was a warm and sunny day.

The scene was unsettling, but Inspector Denny was longing for some food and the comfort of one of the tents. When the rain beat down upon him even harder, he decided to make a run for the camp. The moment he left the tree line and entered the clearing, however, the man found himself wrapped in a cocoon of flickering, blue electricity. The mysterious force hurled him to the ground and knocked him unconscious. When he eventually regained his senses, he was unable to move. Denny was forced to spend a long period lying helplessly on the ground, while the tempest raged mercilessly over him.

After some time, the Inspector was able to struggle unsteadily to his feet. He took a few slow, painful steps in the direction of the camp, and then stopped. He was stunned by the realization that there no longer was a camp. Every tent, every animal, every man, woman and child had vanished. There were no voices to be heard, and no reassuring rhythm of drums. It had all disappeared.

At first, Denny suspected that he had been unconscious much longer than he had originally thought. The only explanation could be that the Natives had struck camp and moved on. As Denny entered the campsite and examined the ground, however, he reconsidered. There were no ashes left from the fires, no dung or hoof prints from the horses, and no sign whatsoever that the area had recently been populated by a substantial number of people. The clearing appeared undisturbed by anything other than the extreme elements.

As the storm continued to rage, the Inspector knew that he had to take action. Continuing on to the fort by raft was now impossible, and there was nothing to sustain him where he was. Denny decided that moving on was the best plan, and set out to cover the remaining 15 miles to Fort Walsh on foot. He arrived near midnight, shivering, starving, exhausted and utterly confused by the strange experience that he had had.

The other officers of the fort laughed when they heard the story, and insisted that Denny's imagination had gotten the better of him. The more he analyzed the situation, however, the more convinced he became that there was no rational explanation. Later, he returned upriver with two pack horses and a Native guide. The official reason was that Denny needed to retrieve his abandoned supplies. While this was true, he was more eager to reexamine the Cree campsite.

He found the place easily, despite its different appearance in the calm weather and warm sunshine. There were a few trees split by lightening—evidence of the previous day's tempestuous weather—but the site seemed otherwise undisturbed.

As Inspector Denny surveyed the clearing, he noticed a few fascinating things. There were a number of stone rings, overgrown by grass, suggesting that a camp had existed there long ago. More interesting and disturbing was the discovery of several bleached human bones. There were two skulls among the remains the officer found, one of them so small that it had to have belonged to a child.

When Denny mentioned these facts to his guide, the Native man did not seem surprised. Two generations before, the guide said, a band of Crees had been slaughtered upon the very spot by their traditional enemies, the Blackfoot. Every man, woman and child had been killed. The camp had been burned to the ground, and the horses stolen. It was a well-known story among the Native people, said the guide. He had heard it since he was a young boy.

During the violent electrical storm, did Inspector Denny actually witness a scene from the past? There have been great scientific minds who thought such a concept possible. Thomas Edison, in his later years, became intrigued with the idea of creating a radio that was sufficiently sensitive to pick up sounds from the past. Basing his theory upon the idea that energy, like matter, was indestructible, Edison believed that the vibrations of every sound ever heard continued to exist—they were simply no longer audible to the average human ear.

Inspector Denny never offered a theory to explain his strange experience, but if he had heard Edison's, he might very well have been convinced.

MODERN MYSTERIES

There are those who believe that
for a ghost story to be authentic,
it must be well aged. But the fact is,
spirits appear in modern settings as often
as they do in historical ones.
Some people think that for a ghost story
to be truly chilling, it must take place against
the moody atmosphere of days gone by.
It is quite the contrary. Contemporary tales—
which are often credible, first-hand accounts of
events that occur in situations and venues
familiar to us all— may even frighten more
because they hit so close to home.

These Saskatchewan stories, all of which
take place within the last 30 years,
offer proof that if you're looking for a good
scare, there's no time like the present.

The Green-Eyed Girl

In 1973, hitchhiking was still a popular way to travel. Most young people thought nothing of sticking out their thumbs to get from point A to point B, and many drivers were still willing enough to oblige them. For a 17-year-old boy named Daryl, who lived on his family's farm near Meadow Lake, things were a little different, though. Daryl's parents were wise enough to recognize the danger of being in a vehicle with a stranger, and they strictly forbade their children from ever hitchhiking or picking up hitchhikers. To break the rules was to lose their driving privileges—which meant social death for a rural teenager.

"Usually, it was a pretty easy rule to follow," said Daryl. But there was one incident that qualified as a notably strange exception.

It was a warm night in August, and Daryl had been at a party with a group of his friends. By the time he had taken two of his buddies home and had turned back on the road toward his parents' farm, it was well after 2 AM. Still, Daryl recalls being wide awake.

"I had the truck window rolled down all the way, and I remember smelling the night air and wishing that I had somewhere else to go. There was a full moon, it was beautiful, and I was really up, you know. Really aware of my surroundings."

As Daryl turned a blind corner on the quiet secondary highway, he was alarmed to see that he wasn't the only early-morning traveller. Walking toward him along the shoulder of the road was a young woman.

"She was wearing this sort of flowing, hippie-style dress," said Daryl. "She had long, straight brown hair and bare feet. I remember the bare feet, because I had this fleeting thought that the gravel

Many of Saskatchewan's roads offer nowhere to hide—unless you're a phantom.

must have hurt. But then she looked up at me, and every single thought went out of my head."

For one moment, the girl made eye contact with Daryl. It was a moment that he remembered well, more than 25 years after it occurred.

"She had the most incredible green eyes that I've ever seen. They were beautiful. I mean, they were beautiful. I was in love."

In love or not, Daryl was still a fairly obedient 17-year-old boy who drove on for a few seconds, grappling with his emotions. It didn't take him long to formulate a rationalization.

"I thought that, technically, the girl wasn't hitchhiking, so it might be okay. Also, it would have been miles to walk to the nearest farmhouse, and what if she was in trouble?"

Armed with excuses for breaking his parents' rule, Daryl turned the truck around. He drove to the corner where he had seen the girl, and then past it, and was extremely confused. Although no more than three or four minutes had passed, the lovely young woman was nowhere to be seen. There was really no place for someone to hide along the deserted road that was bordered by fields. Daryl stopped the truck, got out and looked around. The only thing obstructing his view was the high knoll by the turn in the highway, and he had just seen that from both sides. In such a short span of time the girl could not have walked far; still, it was obvious that she was gone. Bewildered and disappointed, Daryl climbed back into the cab of the pickup and turned the truck around. Once more, he rounded the blind corner as he headed home, and once more, he saw her.

"She was in the same place, just walking toward me along the side of the road. I couldn't believe it… she had not been there a couple of minutes earlier." Again, the girl looked up and met Daryl's gaze. Again, he was astounded by the beauty of her green eyes, but this time there was something different about them: they held a flicker of recognition.

"When she looked at me—okay, it was only for a couple of seconds—but she looked amused, or something. And then she got this little smile on her face, and it was just… It wasn't a friendly smile. It wasn't nice. I could just feel the hair on my arms and on the back of my neck standing up, and I can tell you, I was spooked."

Daryl didn't even consider stopping. He hit the gas pedal and sped away, allowing himself only one brief look in the rear view mirror. Behind him, in the moonlight, he could see nothing but road.

It was an experience and a mystery that Daryl would never forget. It wasn't until years later, however, that he recognized how strange one element of his story was. "The moon was bright," he said, "but still, it was night, and that woman was outside my truck, several yards away from me. Each time I saw her, it was only for a few seconds. So how could I have noticed such a small detail as her eye colour? But I still remember those green eyes so vividly."

It is chilling to think of what might have happened, all those years ago, had Daryl offered a ride to the beautiful young woman with the hypnotic emerald gaze.

Vera's Stories

Although it seems that nearly everyone encounters the supernatural at some point in his lifetime, certain people appear to be more sensitive than others. Those individuals are either consciously aware of, or somehow attract, more than their share of first-hand paranormal experiences.

A woman from Prince Albert named Vera is undoubtedly one of these special people. Throughout her life, she has felt particularly sensitive to certain strange phenomena, and has shared some uncanny moments of communication with her loved ones.

Vera has a niece with whom she is especially close. When the girl was an infant, she was very ill and had to be rushed to Saskatoon for emergency surgery. In her home more than 100 miles away, Vera could clearly hear the baby's distressed crying. Later she learned that the crying she had heard happened at the exact time when her tiny niece had been left, screaming and alone, in an examining room.

Another instance came about following the passing of Vera's mother. The elderly woman had been blind and disabled, and relied on the telephone to keep track of her family. Vera was accustomed to receiving a call from her mom every day at 5:25 PM. Mysteriously, the woman's death did not interrupt that routine. For a long time after the funeral, Vera's telephone would still ring at precisely 5:25 PM. If she tried to answer it there would be no one there, but Vera always knew that the caller was her mother.

One of Vera's most profound supernatural experiences resulted from her brief encounter with a woman whose name she did not even know. It happened during a time that was particularly stressful for Vera. Among the many worries she had were her mother's deteriorating health and the conditions of the extended care facility in which she had been placed.

"My mother was in a home for six years before she died. It was not a home that anyone would want to be in—it could be very abusive," Vera recalled. In an effort to improve her mother's situation, Vera spent countless hours with her, and on most nights she would stay very late to make certain that her mom was comfortably asleep. On one such evening, as Vera tiptoed quietly out past the centrally located nursing station, she felt inexplicably drawn to a certain corridor.

"I had just passed this area when BANG! something stopped me. I was drawn to this other wing, just pulled to this other wing. So I thought, 'Well, why am I here?' Everything was very dark and quiet and still, just like a morgue. Then I heard this crying, just like a child. So I went to this dimly lit room where a woman was lying on her back. She'd had a stroke; she couldn't move. On the wall were pictures of Christ; she was a very Christian lady. But she was crying. I just felt such compassion, so I went into her room and over to her bed and I said, 'Are you all right? Can I get something for you?' Of course, she couldn't answer. So I said, 'I think you're just lonesome.' So I held her hand, and I said, 'You know, you're never alone when the Lord is with you,' and I sang a couple of hymns and I said a couple of prayers with her. Then she calmed right down, and I could tell in her eyes that she was happy I was there. So I talked to her for quite a while, and then I said, 'Now I must go, but I'll come back to see you.' And I left. She seemed comfortable and quiet, so I left. And the next morning when I went to the home, I found out that she had died.

"That was in the summer. In the fall of the same year, I was still under a lot of stress and very tired, because I was doing a lot of cooking and canning. So one morning, I slept in a bit, and I had this dream—it was so vivid, I could never forget it. In the dream,

I was in my kitchen, looking out the window, when I saw something flying at about a 45-degree angle off the horizon. And I'm a fanatic about airplanes, helicopters and that sort of thing, so I was watching it very closely. And I saw it coming closer and closer and closer, until finally it was just outside my kitchen window. Then I could see that it was a chariot of old, with three people in it, and Jesus was driving. When I realized this, I was just so excited.

"The chariot sat just above the ground; it didn't touch the ground. I was just overcome, I was so happy, I couldn't speak. And when I went out to greet them, they didn't speak to me, either. So I was just looking at this vision, when they all got out and stood on my lawn. This one woman with grey hair and a white cloak came over and hugged me. Just a fond hug. Then they all got into the chariot and they left. Just like that."

Vera felt uplifted by the dream, but was mystified about it for quite some time. Then, several weeks later, she happened to mention it to a friend who had done some extensive work in dream studies. The man listened to the details of the dream and connected it to the woman that Vera had comforted in the nursing home. "That's who came to thank you," he said.

The realization was absolutely energizing for Vera. "I was so overwhelmed that year," she said. "I had so much to do, and that dream was like an incentive. Kind of a pat on the back, if you will. I had been sort of depressed and tired, and it did really brighten my spirits. For months, all I had to do was think of that and I was rarin' to go again."

The vision offered proof of how therapeutic it is to know that one is appreciated. It may even have offered proof of communication from the other side. For Vera, however, it was simply a beautiful and vivid experience that she would never forget.

The Phantom Phone Calls

In 1990, a 40-year-old divorced woman named Brenda moved to Yorkton with her two teenaged daughters. They rented a three-bedroom bungalow in a quiet neighbourhood and started their new lives. Brenda settled into her job at a local hotel, and the girls attended school and made friends. There were times, in fact, when Brenda felt that her daughters had entirely too many friends.

"Girls that age—they were 14 and 17—are on the phone a lot," Brenda said, with the voice of experience. "There were times I'd try to phone home, to check on them, after school. All I'd get for hours was a busy signal." Brenda's daughters, who were outgoing and friendly, received as many calls as they made. Evenings were routinely punctuated by the sound of the ringing telephone, and the sisters racing each other to answer it. "It got to the point where I made some rules limiting phone time, and I had the girls tell their friends that they were not to call here after 9:30 PM."

One night, not long after the telephone rules were implemented, the phone rang at 11 PM. Brenda stumbled out of bed and put on her robe. By the time she got to the hallway, she could hear her older daughter saying "goodbye," and hanging up the receiver. Annoyed at having been wakened, Brenda demanded to know who had called. Her daughter replied that it had been a wrong number. "Are you sure?" Brenda asked, suspiciously. The girl was indignant.

"Of course I'm sure!" she replied. "It was some man looking for someone named Charlotte. He sounded pretty confused. I think he might have been drunk."

Two weeks later, the girl's story was confirmed when the same disoriented man called again. This time, the younger daughter answered. As Brenda set the table for dinner, she could hear the girl patiently explaining, "No, there's no one here by that name. No, I'm not Charlotte... What number were you trying to dial?" Brenda went into the living room and took the phone from her daughter's hand.

"Who's calling, please?" she spoke into the receiver, but found that the caller was no longer there. The line had gone dead.

It was around that time that Brenda began to disconnect the phone at night. When she worked the day shift, she had to be on the job at 7 AM, and didn't need any accidental calls disturbing her sleep. For weeks, it was a plan that worked well. Then, in the very early hours of one morning, Brenda was pulled out of a deep sleep by the sound of the ringing phone. She struggled into her bathrobe and swore at herself for forgetting to unplug the cord. As she stumbled down the dark hallway, she vaguely wondered why her daughters weren't out of bed and running to answer the call. It's because the bell sounds strange, she thought. Kind of flat. Maybe it's broken. Brenda sat down in the armchair by the phone table and picked up the receiver, all the while wondering if it might not feel luxurious to have a nonfunctional telephone for a few days. In the midst of her fantasy, she mumbled a sleepy "Hello?"

The voice on the line was distant and toneless. "Charlotte?"

"Who is this?" Brenda found that her telephone etiquette was lacking at 3 AM.

"Charlotte?" The man sounded more faint, the second time. Before Brenda could respond, it was obvious that the call was over. There had been a low hum on the line that ended abruptly.

Brenda leaned over and hung up the phone. She then reached behind the table to unplug the set from the wall jack, and froze. After a moment, she traced her fingers down the dangling telephone cord, to the small plastic plug on the end. The phone had not been connected after all.

There was no sleep for Brenda the rest of that night. A few hours later, at the breakfast table, she sounded as casual as possible when she asked her daughters if they had heard the phone ring during the night. Both shook their heads, no. Brenda said nothing else to the girls, but that same day she had their number changed and their phone set replaced.

Thankfully, there were no more calls.

Several years later, after the girls began attending university in Regina and Brenda had moved into a small condominium, there was a reminder of the eerie incident. At a work-related social function, Brenda was introduced to someone who had once lived in the neighbourhood where she had rented the bungalow. When she described the location of the house, the man nodded in recognition. "I know the place," he said. "You were living in Charlotte's and Ben's old house. I heard that she sold it, just after he died." The colour drained from Brenda's face as she realized what must have happened.

"It was so strange, but obvious," she later said. "This woman named Charlotte sold her house and moved without leaving a forwarding number for her poor, departed hubby."

It makes one wonder if the people who inherited Brenda's old telephone number ever receive strange calls in the middle of the night.

The Hobo

Gary grew up in a small town in southern Saskatchewan. As with all small towns in southern Saskatchewan, it was built around the local grain elevator, and the tall structure's central location made it a perfect meeting place for a boy and his group of friends.

"There was a vacant lot just across the tracks from the elevator, so we'd hang out there sometimes. It was a good place to play ball, although we never had enough kids for a real game. Sometimes a train would come by. It wasn't exciting, but it was kind of a place to call our own," Gary recalled.

There was one summer when, for a brief time, the unofficial playground was the location of some excitement. It was 1979, the year Gary turned ten.

"I remember that it had been a real hot day, but we all wanted to hang around outside by the elevator, anyway. We'd just pant like dogs, but we wouldn't stop playing to go inside," Gary said. "About three o'clock in the afternoon, a train pulled through town. We stopped doing whatever we were doing and ran over to sit by the tracks. That was the biggest thrill we ever had to look forward to—sitting just a few feet away from a moving train. Anyway, we sat and watched for ages, while the cars rolled past. After every one, we'd get this little flash of scenery from the other side. And then, finally, the caboose went by. And that's when we saw the guy."

"The guy" was a man, roughly 40 or 50 years of age. He stood directly across from the boys, facing them, on the other side of the train tracks. His clothing was dirty and ragged, and he wore an old-fashioned cap pulled down low to shade his eyes. The man's hands were stuffed into the front pockets of his shapeless coat.

In 1979, a group of young boys encountered an unsavoury character near a prairie grain elevator.

He regarded the group of wide-eyed children for a moment, then turned and walked away. He disappeared around the corner of the elevator.

"That's when we got up and ran," remembered Gary. "He scared the hell out of us, for a couple of reasons. First, just because he was an adult and he was staring us down. When you're ten, you're always half-expecting some grownup to tell you to get the hell away from something, or stop making a mess, or stop tramping on the grass, or whatever. But later, when my buddies and I started talking about it, we thought the way he just showed up was kind of creepy, too."

It did seem odd that the boys never sensed the man's approach, even though they had a brief view of the area after each passing railway car. The stranger's layers of apparel were suspiciously inappropriate for such a sweltering day. And there was one other thing.

"We all agreed that he looked kind of, I guess, out of time, or something. We'd all heard lectures and warnings about mysterious strangers, but this guy looked like the Waltons' version of a creep, not ours."

The boys talked about the strange man on and off for days. As Gary would explain later, "the excitement more than made up for the scare." But what the friends didn't know was that they were about to be scared, again.

It was a cool, damp evening about two weeks after the first occasion. Steady rain during the day had made playing outside impossible, but the skies had cleared by late afternoon, and the kids were out making up for lost time after supper. A group of six or seven were making canals in a large patch of mud near the tracks, when one boy happened to look up.

"I don't remember what he said," Gary admitted, "but it made us all stop and look. And there he was again. We just froze."

Again, the filthy, dishevelled stranger stood directly across the tracks from where the boys played. Again, he paralyzed them with his vacant stare. But this time, he smiled at them. It was the most horrible smile Gary ever remembered seeing.

"It wasn't friendly, it was… menacing. His teeth were disgusting. They were black with rot, and some were missing. I remember standing there, just shaking. It's a wonder I didn't wet myself."

After a moment or two, when the boys were thoroughly weak with fear, the stranger turned around and walked away. Once more, he vanished around the corner of the grain elevator and did not return.

"I wish now that we would have followed and taken a look around that corner, but there was no way that we had the guts to do it, then. I don't think we moved for, like, ten minutes," Gary later laughed. When the kids did move, it was to get home before darkness fell. For the next week, none of them felt like playing in the vacant lot or watching the activity around the railway tracks.

Eventually, the fear faded, and a few of the kids did reclaim their play area. They did so only when the reassuring warmth of the afternoon sun could be felt on their shoulders, however. Gary remembers that, during that time, there wasn't a single suggestion to meet there after supper. "The days were long," he explained, "but no way did we want to run the risk of being there at dusk. And it was just too deserted in the evenings. We wouldn't chance it." And so the kids continued to play, as long as they were reassured by the occasional passing vehicle and the distant sounds of activity around the elevator. Then one day, Gary had an idea.

"I was watching some guys working by the main entrance to the elevator. I don't know what they were doing—to this day, I don't know exactly what went on there, despite the amount of time I spent hanging around. Anyway, the sun was out and I was feeling brave, so I told my friends that I was going to go talk to this guy. And I did."

Gary crossed the tracks and tried to exude confidence as he approached the workers. His friends watched from the vacant lot, full of respect and curiousity. The men, absorbed in their task, did not even notice the sunburned kid walking purposefully toward them. Gary had to pull himself up to his full height and say "excuse me" twice to gain their attention. The one fellow kept working. The other, seemingly in charge, stopped and asked Gary what he wanted.

"I told him I was just curious about something," Gary recalled. "I said that there was this guy we had seen around here a couple of times, and maybe he knew him. And then I described the stranger."

Gary will always remember the man's reaction to his query.

"He went pale. I mean, *white*, with little red patches on his cheeks. And all he said to me was, 'Don't you kids ever, ever go near that guy. Don't talk to him, and don't follow him.' And that was that."

The man's warning never to follow the stranger gave Gary an idea. While he was over by the grain elevator, he thought he might as well take a look around the corner of the building where the man always disappeared. What he saw puzzled him.

"There was about ten feet of room to walk, but then you ran into a big, high, chicken-wire fence that enclosed a storage area. And that fence jutted out and joined up with the one that ran parallel to the grain elevator. So once you got around the corner, there was nowhere to go."

By the time Gary finished his investigation and walked back across the tracks, his friends were beside themselves with curiousity. Gary told them about the elevator employee's reaction to his question, and about what he saw around that one corner. Then he offered them a conclusion.

"I said, 'you know, I think we saw a ghost.' Nobody disagreed with me. It was a little too weird to be anything else."

Months later, when the friends were all back in school and the summer's adventure had become a memory, Gary discovered what he thought might be a clue to the frightening phantom's identity.

"I was in Social Studies, and we were having a discussion about the Dirty Thirties. The teacher started telling us about these hobos who rode the rails across the country, and how they had nothing, and they were like bums on the move. I thought about the guy we had seen by the tracks, and I thought, yeah, he was a hobo!"

Gary and his friends never saw the ghost again. Of course, they never went looking for him.

"Once would have been enough," laughed Gary. "Twice was interesting, but I didn't need a third experience. Honestly, I wouldn't even want to run into this character today."

It makes one wonder if the scruffy spirit is still lingering in the same small town, looking for someone to frighten by the tracks. Perhaps he is, or perhaps he's moved on, riding the rails and haunting whichever stop he happens to make on his lonely journey through the afterlife.

Ghostly Knock
On Ginger

Julie remembers the first day she moved into her small, older home in Prince Albert.

"I was unpacking boxes, trying to get things put away, and there was this pounding on the door." The young woman ran from the back bedroom to see who it was, hoping it might be some friends arriving to offer a bit of help. When she threw open the door, however, there was no one to be seen. "I figured it was kids," she recalled, "and just got back to work."

A half-hour later, the same loud knocking caught Julie in the midst of setting up her bed frame. It took her a minute or two to untangle herself from the project and make her way to the door. The banging continued nearly nonstop until Julie got to the door, but when she opened it, once again she found nobody standing there. Thinking that the pranksters couldn't have run far, she searched the bushes in the front yard, and peered over the neighbours' fences. She found nothing, heard no tell-tale giggling, and had hours of work ahead of her, so Julie quickly gave up her search and walked back into the house.

The instant she closed the door, the pounding began.

"I was standing right there, so I yanked it open, ready to say 'Gotcha!' But there was no one on the step. That's when I got a little chill. But I just said, 'Okay, whoever you are, knock it off. I have a lot to do, today.' And that was it for quite awhile."

Julie's door-knocking ghost still visits on a fairly regular basis, but she has found a way to get around the nuisance of it. "I had a doorbell installed, and I put up a sign that says, 'Ring the bell if you're serious.' That way, if I'm busy and the ghost knocks on the door, I can comfortably ignore it."

It's been a simple solution to a spectral problem in Prince Albert.

The Bat Lady

The boys called her "the Bat Lady." Not to her face of course, but behind her back, when they were grumbling about having been chased away from her property yet again. They were often forced to abandon a ball that had gone over her high, weathered fence. Had they been bigger boys—sixth-graders, say—they might have cursed the old woman more colourfully. But the oldest among them was only nine, and they were all pretty good kids who still listened to their parents on such issues as swearing. So they simply called her the Bat Lady, because of the black clothing she wore and the way she fluttered her hands and screeched at them when she came running out of the house.

The only reason that they ever encountered the strange old crone was that one of the gang, a fair-haired boy named Howard, lived across the back alley from her. Howard had the biggest back-yard in which to play, so most of the hot Regina summer afternoons were spent there. Over the course of several summers, great wars were waged with water pistols, intricate roads were built for a battered and motley collection of Hot Wheels cars, and the World Series was won, sometimes weekly, despite the crippling fact that the boys seldom had more than a total of two or three players per team. Even more limiting was the fact that Howard's mother, who was generous with the popsicles but adamant about rules, insisted that they use only lightweight, plastic balls and aim them away from the glass patio doors. This left the boys hitting pop flies at the back fence. If the ball went over the fence, it had to be retrieved from the alley. If it cleared two fences, they were at the mercy of the Bat Lady.

On one particular afternoon when the kids were forced to sneak into the woman's overgrown backyard, they hadn't even been playing baseball. There were only four of them that day, so they had opted for a lively game of Starsky and Hutch instead. The famous police duo (played, on this day, by Howard and his friend Mike) was in hot pursuit of two hardened criminals. As they wove dangerously around the swing set, one of the wily crooks thought it wise to toss the evidence—and did. It sailed over the fence, across the alley filled with garbage cans and dandelions, and into the Bat Lady's backyard. It was bad news, indeed, for the evidence had actually been one of Mike's brand-new tennis shoes. He had taken them off, thinking his parents might be upset if the shoes got all grass-stained. He was even more certain of their reaction if he was to arrive home with only one left. Given the seriousness of the situation, the boys abandoned their game and sat down in the grass to work out a plan.

There was no point in asking Howard's mother for help. Another of her rules was that they could play boisterously, as long as they never bothered the neighbours. The boys briefly considered a mature approach, such as knocking on the Bat Lady's front door and explaining the unfortunate situation, but decided there had been too much past ugliness to try that. In the end, they all agreed that a stealthy recovery mission was their only option. Howard was the best fence-climber present on that day and therefore was elected for the job.

Howard's heart was pounding under his thin T-shirt as he crossed the narrow alley. The trick, he knew from past experience, was not so much getting into the old lady's yard as it was getting out of it. It was harder to look for good footholds on the splintered, grey boards when a crazy person was bearing down on you, flapping her claw-like hands and screaming things you could never understand. With that in mind, Howard stopped at the fence and took a moment to plan his moves very carefully.

By peeking through the narrow spaces between the boards, he was able to see where Mike's gleaming white tennis shoe had landed. It was in the garden patch, by the struggling, parched tomato plants. That wasn't great: people tended to get twice as mad about a kid trampling their garden as they did about a kid trespassing on their scrubby lawn. Still, the shoe was fairly close to the fence, so it would be a quick job to snatch it and run. Getting back over the high fence was the only niggling detail to work out. Howard scanned the back portion of the yard, looking for anything that might serve as a stepping stool. He found something better when his eye spied the latch for the back gate.

The Bat Lady's back gate could only be opened from the inside, but that suited Howard's purpose perfectly. All he needed was a means of quick escape, and now he had one. Being a thorough boy, and a fairly frightened one, he took a moment to familiarize himself with the mechanism. The hinges were on the inside, so the gate opened inward. It was a simple lift-and-pull latch. This will be easy, Howard told himself, and crawled up on the tallest trash can. In fact, it will be a piece of cake, he thought, as he stepped up onto the fence and jumped down into the grass. It wasn't.

Howard landed badly, twisting his right foot beneath him in the dry grass. He said a word he knew he wasn't allowed to say, then slowly stood up and took a couple of careful steps. No permanent damage, he decided, and limped into the garden to retrieve the lost shoe. He bent over to pick it up, when suddenly there were three shoes. Mike's white runner, which had lain alone among the thirsty plants and cracked, grey earth, was now flanked by two filthy black oxfords. Terrified, Howard looked up. His gaze was met directly by the Bat Lady's.

She stood in the garden like a horrible scarecrow, her long, matted hair hanging over her puckered, toothless face. Her eyes were bright with fury, and she raised one gnarled hand to point accusingly at Howard. The menacing motion was all that was necessary to set the boy in motion.

Desperately, he ran for the far corner of the yard, his eyes set upon the life-saving gate latch. He knew the hag was behind him; he could hear her shrill, incomprehensible complaints. At one point, her bony, yellow fingers caught a shred of his T-shirt. Fuelled by terror, Howard put out an extra burst of speed and freed himself. Finally, he reached the gate, opened the latch, and pulled. To his absolute horror, only the top of the gate bent with his force. Panicked, the boy looked down to see the small detail which he had overlooked before: the aged fence and gate had settled deep into the ground. It couldn't be opened. He was trapped. Panting with fear, Howard spun around to face the Bat Lady.

She was gone.

The boy was stunned, disbelieving. She couldn't have gone back to the house that quickly, and there was no place to hide. It had to be a trick, and Howard spun around anxiously, scanning every corner of the backyard. It was as empty as it had been before he had hopped the fence, a fact that frightened him even more. Howard quickly decided that later would be a good time to analyze the details, and pulled an empty milk crate over to the fence. He tossed Mike's shoe over, then used the crate to boost himself up. Howard dropped down into the alley on his throbbing ankle, and turned to see his friends watching, wide-eyed, through a narrow opening in his own back gate.

They all wanted to know what had happened. Once he was in the familiar safety of his own yard and his breath was coming more evenly, he told them. To his dismay, the dramatic story was met with more confusion than respect. They hadn't heard the Bat Lady, they insisted, and when she got screeching, you could normally hear her up and down the block. And anyway, they all wanted to know why Howard had dropped into the backyard if she had been standing right there in the garden?

Howard froze. That was the frightening detail that he hadn't been able to put his finger on a few minutes earlier. The Bat Lady *hadn't* been standing in the garden or anywhere else in the backyard. He would have seen her before he went over the fence. He felt a little bit sick. The other three kept asking him questions such as what did she smell like, that close up? Howard didn't answer. He thrust the rescued shoe at Mike, and said he had to go inside for the rest of the afternoon. The boys, perplexed, eventually drifted away to find other activities. Howard found the cool refuge of his bedroom and didn't emerge until his mother called him for dinner.

It would normally have been noticed that Howard was quite subdued at the table, but that night his mother and father were too absorbed in their own conversation. Something about the police being somewhere, the middle of the night before, and the poor relative who found someone. Howard's mother in particular kept her voice low and respectful, and clucked her tongue at regular intervals. When Howard's sister, Wendy, asked, "Well how *long* had she been there and were there any bugs?" she was silenced by a look from their father. Howard paid attention to none of it. He was interested only in clearing enough of his plate so that he would be allowed to retreat to his room.

Two hours later, Howard was lying on his bed, bouncing a little rubber ball off the wall and still trying to make sense of his afternoon. He couldn't understand how the Bat Lady could have appeared out of nowhere. Even more confusing was the way she had vanished: one moment he had felt her grotesque fingers snagging his shirt and heard her shrill screech in his ears, and the next moment she was nowhere to be seen. And the other guys hadn't heard her shrieking. How could they not have heard her?

The question was fresh in Howard's mind when Wendy walked into his room. She rapped twice on the door as she opened it, which was her skimpy acknowledgement of his right to privacy. Howard was too tired to complain, and simply looked at her. She was clearly bursting with some bit of information.

Wendy tried waiting to have the news coaxed out of her, but nearly ruptured with the effort. She tried to bait Howard by saying that she had overheard their parents talking in the den. He showed no particular interest. Finally, she spilled the whole story. There were bugs, she said, there had to have been. Dad said he figured she had been there for days and days, maybe more than a week, before anyone found her. Wendy concluded with a comment that the whole thing was so gross, didn't Howard think it was gross? Howard simply shook his head and explained that he didn't have a clue what Wendy was talking about. The girl stared at him, incredulous.

She wanted to know where Howard had been at dinner, and asked whether he ever listened to anyone? Howard shrugged his shoulders. He was tired of the conversation. He was tired, period, and went back to bouncing his little rubber ball off the wall. Wendy's next sentence made him drop the ball, though; it rolled under the bed, where it would lay, forgotten and dusty, for weeks.

"That old woman across the alley. The crazy one that you and your nerds call the Bat Lady. She's *dead*," Wendy nearly shouted. "She's been dead for ages, but no one found her until last night, you moron!" She turned and flounced out of the room, slamming the door behind her.

Howard suddenly felt very cold, and very alone.

The other boys came over as usual, the next day, but Howard told them he didn't feel like playing. He didn't feel like it for several days, and it was several more days before he could be coaxed into playing in his own backyard. Every so often, Howard's parents would look at him, then look at each other and raise their eyebrows questioningly, but they never asked him directly what was wrong. That was good, because it would be about 20 years before Howard felt like talking about it.

Eventually, some new people bought the Bat Lady's house, and they fixed it up and mowed the grass and watered the garden and replaced the sunken, splintered back fence with some shiny new chain-link. It didn't matter to Howard. He never went into that yard again, no matter what went over the fence.

He never felt sure that the Bat Lady, dead or not, would let him back out.

Have Ghost, Will Travel

The mere mention of a haunted home brings several pictures immediately to mind. Most people will imagine something old enough to have a history—a mist-enshrouded manor, a shadowy, Victorian-style abode or, at the very least, a weathered prairie farmhouse. Few would conjure up the image of a mobile home, but on an acreage near Battleford, there is a family who claims to have lived in a haunted trailer.

Lynn and Harvey were beginning the process of building their own home. It was a project that was expected to take more than a year to complete, and they didn't want to commute back and forth between Battleford and their property on a daily basis. They considered tent-living, at least for the summer months, but felt it wouldn't be suitable for their two-year-old daughter, Cherie. In the end, they purchased a trailer, and moved it onto their land. It was outdated and badly showing its age, but provided the young family with an economical and suitable solution to their problem.

Harvey, who was always very safety-conscious, removed the wheels and spent two days securing the trailer on heavy wooden blocks. He then skirted the perimeter with plywood so Cherie wouldn't be tempted to play beneath their temporary home. Still, he was often awakened at night by the sensation of movement. The rocking, rolling feeling of being in a vehicle always stopped the moment he opened his eyes, but was very strange, nonetheless. Harvey attributed it to overwork, and forgot about it.

One night, however, Harvey and Lynn were awakened at the same time, by the same sickening sensation. "The trailer's rolling!"

gasped Lynn as she sat up in bed, clutching the blankets. Harvey noticed with alarm that although he was wide awake, the motion hadn't stopped. Furthermore, Lynn was feeling it, too. Still, he knew it wasn't possible.

"There are no wheels on this thing. We can't be moving," he assured his wife, ignoring the groaning sound the joints in the walls made as they swayed. Harvey jumped out of bed and yanked at the bedroom window curtains. Suddenly everything was still.

The couple nearly swooned with relief as they saw the familiar view, illuminated in dull yellow by the yard light. Lynn quickly checked on Cherie, who had apparently either felt nothing or slept through the whole affair. Harvey opened the back door a crack, and looked down at the ground. The scrubby bits of grass that passed for a lawn were undisturbed. The trailer, obviously, had not moved an inch.

The next day, Harvey and Lynn spent hours talking about the incident. Every time Cherie was out of earshot, they would wonder, in hushed tones, how it could be logically explained. Neither was able to provide an answer.

That night, they went to bed late and still found it difficult to fall asleep. When they did, however, they were allowed to sleep undisturbed until morning. It was nearly two weeks before the trailer decided to roll again, but when it did, it seemed to get up to cruising speed.

As in the previous occurrence, Lynn and Harvey had been sleeping for several hours when it happened. Both were rudely awakened when their home seemed to hit a bump on whichever phantom road it travelled.

"Did you feel that!" yelled Harvey, then quickly realized that Lynn would indeed have felt the movement. It had knocked her right out of bed.

"Check the window! Look out the window!" Lynn begged, as she climbed back up on the mattress and grasped the headboard for stability. Harvey stood up and lurched across the bedroom floor. The curtains were swaying wildly. Harvey tore one halfway off the rod as he lost his balance while trying to pull it open. The view that the ripped fabric exposed wasn't quite as reassuring as it had been the time before.

The familiar trees were there. The familiar jaundiced yard light shone upon them. But somehow, although the scene never changed, it seemed to be rushing into the distance, as if the trailer was moving at an extreme speed. "I'm going to be sick," announced Lynn, and turned her head away from the nauseating optical illusion.

Just then, Cherie began to cry, and Harvey moved shakily down the hall to the toddler's room. Using the walls of the narrow passageway to steady himself, he carried the distraught little girl into the master bedroom. The frightened family of three then sat in the middle of the bed, clutching each other, until the storm of movement stopped. It had been a full 15-minute show.

The next day, Harvey and Lynn drove into Battleford and rented a tiny, one-room apartment. Somehow, driving back and forth to the acreage no longer seemed to be such a hardship, and sharing a small space among the three of them felt cozy, rather than confining. Best of all, the apartment building had a solid foundation and no wheels.

As for the trailer, someone else has it now. Harvey, eager to be rid of it, gave it away to a distant acquaintance. He felt a certain amount of guilt over his lack of disclosure, but soothed his conscience by refusing to accept any money for the haunted home.

It would be interesting to know where the trailer sits now, and if it ever takes its new owners along on eerie nighttime voyages.

Joker's Wild

A woman named Janet who lives on an acreage near Carrot River has long believed her house to be haunted.

"It's never been a scary sort of thing," she said. "Our ghost is like a prankster. He likes to flash the lights on and off, and turn off the television during the last scene of our favourite show, and hide things. Stuff like that. It's never so much that you get annoyed. He's just a friendly spirit, I think, looking for attention. The kids even gave him a name: they call him 'Chester.'"

Chester's benign antics have kept the family amused for a number of years, and only once has he ever strayed from his usual routine. Janet remembers the incident well. It was a weekday morning, and she was preparing to visit a friend.

"It was kind of important," Janet recalled. "My friend had a doctor's appointment, and she couldn't drive herself, so I offered to play chauffeur. And about half an hour before I had to leave, Chester started to act up in a way he never had before."

The phantom pranks began when Janet went to the bathroom to brush her teeth. Her toothbrush, which always sat in a glass in the bathroom cabinet, was missing. Janet searched the other shelves of the cabinet, thinking that another member of the family may have accidentally borrowed it, but could find nothing. When a few minutes had passed, she decided that she would have to borrow her husband's toothbrush, and buy a couple of replacements while she was out. The mystery was not solved, but the problem was—until Janet realized that there was no toothpaste to be found. In frustration, she brushed her teeth with plain cold water and popped a breathmint in her mouth.

Janet had only a few minutes left before she had to be on the road, but was not overly concerned. All she had to do was dress, grab her purse and her car keys, let the cat out of the house, and she'd be on her way. It couldn't possibly take more than a few minutes.

Seconds later, as she reached for the carefully folded outfit that she had left on the foot of the bed, she changed her mind. The clothing had been fine an hour earlier—now it was damp, to the extent that it had even left a small moist patch on the duvet cover. Nothing had been irreparably damaged, but Janet had to find another outfit, which put her several minutes behind schedule.

The practical jokes all bore Chester's trademark playfulness, but Janet's usual patience was wearing paper-thin. "At that point, I had to be out of the house in about 30 seconds, or else I was going to be late," she said. "Chester was normally a one-gag kind of ghost. He'd do some little thing, and then you wouldn't hear from him for days. It was extremely frustrating that he'd chosen this particular morning to put on a whole show."

Frustrating or not, the show was far from over. As Janet quickly dressed in a second outfit, she found that all the pairs of neatly rolled socks in her bureau had been mixed up. There was not one matching pair to be found. Gathering her purse and keys required a five minute search: Janet eventually found both stuffed behind an oversized throw-cushion on her living room sofa. And the cat (who was normally obedient, for a cat) refused to be let outside. The animal crouched stubbornly in the farthest dusty corner under Janet's son's bed, and hissed every time it was spoken to. With one last, desperate look at the clock, Janet decided that it was time to give up.

"I figured if the cat peed on the rug, so be it. I ran out the door and jumped in the car." As Janet jammed the key into the ignition, she was calculating that if she did just a little speeding en route, she would not be too late picking up her friend. That probably would have been the case—except that the car would not start. "I got nothing," Janet later explained. "No grinding, no dead-battery sound, nothing." That was when she realized she would have to abandon her whole mission.

"It was very embarrassing, but I went in and called my friend, and told her that I couldn't make it. It was too late for her to get another ride, so she had to cancel her appointment. I felt really bad about the whole thing, and really angry at Chester. But I didn't say anything."

An hour later, Janet noticed that as soon as she had placed the phone call to her friend, Chester's pranks had stopped. She went about her regular routine without incident. Out of curiousity, she went to the bathroom and peeked into the cabinet. Her toothbrush and toothpaste sat in their usual places. She then took her car keys off the hook on the wall and went out to the driveway. She opened the door of her blue Taurus and put the key in the ignition.

"It started on the first turn," Janet said. "Not a thing wrong with it."

In the days that followed, Janet spent a great deal of time considering her strange morning with Chester. In the end, she decided that there had been some important reason the ghost had not wanted her to go.

"I'll never know for sure, but maybe I would have had an accident on the highway," she speculated. "There was definitely something different about that day."

Following his mysterious flurry of activity, Chester went back to his usual tricks. Janet's attitude toward the spirit had changed, however. She would later sum it up by saying, "I just appreciated Chester more. Nowadays, I think I'm very lucky to have a ghost who plays harmless little jokes—and looks out for me."

When it comes to hauntings, you can't ask for better than that.

The Abandoned Church

Anyone who has spent his teenage years in a small farming community knows that the environment can be a bit socially restrictive. A young man named Dustin who recently graduated and moved away from his family home in northwestern Saskatchewan can sum it up in two sentences:

"In the winter, nobody does much," Dustin said. "In the summer, there are bush parties."

Large parties meant dozens of people and a huge bonfire in some out-of-the-way location. Sometimes, though, a warm summer night just meant that Dustin and a couple of buddies would take a six pack and go for a drive. On these occasions, they often ended up turning off the highway and onto the overgrown piece of property that was home to a decrepit and abandoned old church. There they would play the car stereo and "shoot the shit" until the beer and conversation ran out. They never for one moment considered going inside the church.

"It was such a wreck, we thought we'd probably go right through the floor if we stepped inside," said Dustin. "But… also, it was a church, and you have to have some respect for that. Mostly, though, we didn't want to go in because of all the stories."

The stories that Dustin was familiar with told of the old church being haunted. A caretaker had hanged himself in the belfry, the legend said, and ever since, people who glanced up through the broken timbers of the tower at night reported seeing mysterious lights flitting about. It was the caretaker, storytellers whispered, trying to lure someone into the church to keep him company.

Mysterious lights could sometimes be seen flickering through the broken timbers of the abandoned church.

"We always talked about the ghost, and we were superstitious enough to stay out of the church, but I don't think any of us ever believed it," said Dustin.

That changed in the summer of 1998.

"It was a nice, warm night, but it was like a Wednesday, or something, so nothing was going on." Dustin had been driving around with a friend. When they got bored, they decided to visit the old church. The sun had set, and twilight was quickly bleeding out of the sky by the time they parked the car in their usual spot.

"We turned on some tunes, and we were just leaning against the car, talking," Dustin explained. "And we had a couple cans of pop—we weren't drinking at all that night, so you can't blame what we saw on that. Anyway, we were there, and we were facing the bell tower, and all of a sudden there was this light."

The light that Dustin and his friend saw began as a muted, nearly orange glow that emanated from the belfry window. "We thought it was a fire," Dustin said, "and we thought we should get the hell out of there, so no one would think we set it." The young men were too fascinated to leave, however, and watched as the light shrunk into a small, luminescent orb. The radiant globe moved in slow and deliberate patterns before their eyes, then dropped downward out of sight. The faintest hint of orange illumination could then be detected in the main floor windows of the church.

"My friend wanted to go and check it out," said Dustin, "but I wouldn't let him. The fact was, I wanted to go looking for it, too. I had this really strong urge to just walk right in there. I think that was the scariest part of it."

Dustin and his friend resisted the urge to investigate, and drove back to town in a hurry. Along the way, they talked nonstop about what they had seen.

"We were trying to figure out if it could have been reflected light, or anything like that. Headlights from the highway, maybe. But we couldn't come up with an explanation that made sense. The thing is, even now, we don't know what we saw. But it was weird."

The experience was so strange, in fact, that Dustin and his friend never spoke of it to anyone but each other.

"The story came up once in a while, at parties, but we just kept quiet. We didn't want to be seen as the two psychos who actually thought they saw the ghost."

Which makes one wonder: how many people truly have seen the ghost in the old abandoned church, but have chosen to remain silent? In this small, quiet, rural community, no one will ever know for sure.

A Spirit on the Stairs

A man named Paul bought an older home in Weyburn in 1987. He knew he was getting a two-storey, Victorian-style "fixer-upper" with a great deal of character and potential. He did not know that he was also getting a ghost.

"I suppose I should have figured it out earlier than I did, but you never expect something like that," Paul explained. "I expected old wiring, so when the lights would flash on and off, I'd attribute it to that. I expected that the house would have creaks and groans in the structure, so I didn't worry too much about the weird noises I heard." Paul also expected that restoring the home to its former charm would take a lot of time and effort, so he ignored the various strange incidents that took place and got down to work.

Every evening and most weekends, Paul spent his time stripping gaudy wallpaper and mildewy carpets, and repairing crumbling plaster and decaying woodwork. It was hard work, but mainly cosmetic, until he decided to make one major change.

"There was a narrow little staircase in the back of the house that led from the kitchen to the upstairs hall. Someone had walled it over years before, and I decided to open it up again."

When Paul put his sledgehammer through the wall at the bottom of the staircase, he released decades of musty air, cobwebs and something inexplicable. That night as he lay in bed, he finally heard a noise that could not be dismissed as the creaking timbers of an old home. It was the sound of heavy, deliberate footsteps ascending the newly opened rear staircase.

"It was so real, I thought someone had broken into the house,"

Paul recalled. Quickly and quietly, he jumped out of bed and looked for the heaviest weapon he could find. The best he could produce was a metal three-hole punch that had been sitting on the desk in his bedroom. Armed with his deadly office implement, Paul stood by the door, ready to strike. The footsteps reached the top of the stairs—and stopped.

"I was sweating, I can tell you. I stood there for I don't know how long, waiting for this guy to take a few more steps down the hall, or go back down the stairs. But there was nothing. It was just absolutely quiet."

After a while, Paul began to feel foolish, waiting for the attack that would not come. He dared to open the bedroom door a crack, and peered down the hallway. He could see nothing. He ventured out into the hall, and walked to the top of the rear staircase. Nothing. Paul decided that a thorough check of the house could wait until morning, and returned to bed.

"But I didn't sleep much," he admitted.

The next morning, nothing in the house was amiss. Even stranger, the only footprints disturbing the years of dust on the rear stairs appeared to be Paul's own. He knew what he had heard the night before, however, and didn't question his senses. That morning, for the first time, Paul began to reassess many of the odd little occurrences that had taken place in the house.

"I started to think that maybe I didn't misplace things as often as I thought I did. And maybe the old wiring wasn't to blame every time the lights went on or off by themselves. It was very strange… but I thought I had a ghost."

If that was the case, the spirit was at least easy to get along with. Nothing it did was ever frightening or threatening. The footsteps on the stairs had only been so unsettling because Paul hadn't expected to hear them, on that first night. Afterward, however, he took them in stride.

"I'd just think, okay, that's my buddy walking upstairs again. There was really nothing scary about it. I'd roll over and go to sleep."

As Paul's renovation neared completion, the ghostly activity became less and less prevalent. The week that the staircase was first opened up, Paul heard phantom footsteps on four separate occasions. By the time he had refinished the area, the phenomenon was happening no more than once every ten days or so. While he restored the damaged hardwood floors and put fresh paint on the walls, he was constantly frustrated by misplaced tools and brushes. As he did the final touch-ups, however, everything seemed to be staying in place. As for the lights that turned on and off of their own volition—well, that still happens.

"The wiring got completely redone, right up to code," reported Paul, "but the ghost still likes to play with lights. I don't mind. It's not particularly disruptive, and all the annoying activity has stopped."

Perhaps it's a sign of appreciation for all of Paul's meticulous work, from a tenant of the old house who has decided to stay on indefinitely.

PHANTOMS IN THE FAMILY

*Many of the ghost sightings
on record are cases in which the
witness recognized the apparition
as a departed family member.
More often than not, these spirits
have a reason for returning:
they want to say goodbye,
provide some information,
offer a warning or provide a
sense of comfort.*

*Read on, and discover some
of the things that can happen
when relatives return from
the other side.*

Nora's Notebook

It was a picture-perfect summer day. The sun was shining warmly from the clearest of deep blue skies, and a light breeze kept the heat from becoming uncomfortable. Marjorie thought, not for the first time that day, that she should be outdoors, staking her tomato plants or weeding the flower beds. Instead, she was rummaging through the dusty storage space beneath the basement stairs, wiping rivulets of perspiration from her forehead and feeling like an intruder in her own house. The sensation of invading someone's privacy stemmed from the fact that these were not Marjorie's things stored in the dark cubby beneath the creaking boards. They were Nora's.

Nora had been Hank's first wife. She had been dead for nearly six years; it had been four already when Marjorie had married the lonely widower and come to live on the little farm near Belle Plaine. But it hadn't taken Marjorie long to discover that while four years showed sufficient respect for the dead, it was not long enough to erase their memory. She was constantly haunted by Hank's reminders of his late wife's domesticity. Nora used to knit for all the grandkids, and Nora had always dried the sheets and towels out on the line because it made them smell so nice. She had kept up the house so well that he hadn't known what dust was until she passed away, he'd say, and in the summer there had been fragrant little bouquets of flowers in every room.

Marjorie knew that Hank didn't mean to be insensitive, but the constant comparisons stung. Worst of all were the reminiscences of Nora's culinary abilities. Marjorie had always considered herself to be a fair cook, but now, three times a day, she had to brace herself for the inevitable comment that her predecessor made the pie with a little more cinnamon, or the scrambled eggs with a little more cream, or had a knack for homemade bread that no one else could match. It was unbearable.

One day, Marjorie's step-daughter came by the house with a special request. She wanted to borrow her mother's cookbook. Marjorie told her to help herself to any of the books on the wide kitchen shelf, but the young woman shook her head. Not those, she said. The little one. The hardcover notebook where her mother had written all of her special recipes. Marjorie rifled through the various books, but could find nothing matching the description. The step-daughter, who had been hoping to duplicate her mother's famous pickled preserves, went away disappointed. Marjorie was left with a nagging curiousity.

If the notebook had not been given to the daughter, she reasoned, it had to be somewhere still in the house. And if Marjorie could find it, she might at least be able to deflect a portion of the criticism that assaulted her daily. Systematically, she began to search the house, looking for the little book that would make her as good a cook as Nora had been.

The clothing and linen closets were examined quickly and easily. Marjorie found nothing, but wasn't surprised. She simply felt that she might as well eliminate the easiest possibilities, first. Under the pretense of spring cleaning, every drawer and shelf in the large, bright kitchen was cleared out and reorganized. The result was satisfying, but the notebook did not turn up. Eventually, Marjorie knew she would have to go through the hot, dark storage area beneath the basement stairs. Her skin crawled at the thought of the spider webs and mouse droppings she was sure to find, but it was the only place left to look. And she knew that many of Nora's personal belongings were in the tightly packed cardboard boxes there. She chose a day when she knew that Hank would be out in the fields for hours, and set to work.

It was a frustrating job, and an uncomfortable one. Marjorie lived with enough daily reminders of Nora, without sorting through her correspondence and hair ornaments and well-thumbed paperbacks. Box after box of such items was pulled from the sweltering space, opened, and unpacked. Box after box was set aside to be wrestled back into the hole, once Marjorie had examined its contents. After several disappointing hours, Marjorie happened to glance at her wristwatch. The watch told her that it was late, nearly 3:30 PM. The grime on her arms and hands told her that she would need a shower before Hank came in from the fields and asked her what on earth she'd been up to, to get so filthy. Marjorie performed a quick mental calculation and decided that she had time to search through one more carton.

In it, she struck gold.

There, beneath a quilted tissue-box holder upon which Nora had embroidered her name in a great flourish of purple thread, sat a notebook. The fat, pink cabbage roses on the book's cloth cover were yellowed with age and stained with small drops of food. This had to be what she was looking for. Marjorie held her breath and carefully opened the book to its first, lined page. At the very top, in Nora's spidery script, were the words "Raisin-Drop Cookies." Marjorie let her breath out in a great whoosh, and smiled. For the first time in two years, she felt that she might be getting a break.

After stuffing the cardboard cartons back into the storage space and having a quick shower, Marjorie put together a little supper. There was sliced cold ham, tomatoes and potato salad. Hank said it was good, but Nora always put a bit of dill in her salad, he thought. Marjorie only smiled, and thought of the book, which was now tucked safely into her make-up drawer. She was sure that Hank was soon to become more appreciative of her cooking.

The next morning, when Hank was out in the farthest field, Marjorie pulled the notebook from its hiding place. She thumbed through it, noting that there was no particular method of organization to it. It seemed that Nora had simply added in her favourite recipes as she came upon them, sometimes going back at a later date to note some adjustment. "Rises better if the milk is warmed" was jotted into the margin of one page. "Can substitute applesauce for 1/2 veg. oil" had been scrawled on the bottom of another. Occasionally, there were menu suggestions. "Good with creamed peas and carrots and quick-rise buns" was noted beneath Nora's famous meatloaf recipe. Marjorie scanned the list of ingredients quickly. She had everything needed for that dish, and decided to serve it for supper that evening. Happily, she replaced the book in her drawer, and began to plan her day. Before leaving the bedroom, she grabbed a sweater from the closet. Despite the morning sunshine, she felt uncomfortably chilled.

As she watched Hank eat his evening meal, Marjorie felt that all the hard work of the previous day had been worth it. He made appreciative sounds as he worked his way through the meatloaf, which was wrapped around an ingenious centre stuffing of bread crumbs and melted cheddar. The warm rolls were used to mop up every last drop of glistening, seasoned cream left behind from the vegetables. When at last he pushed his chair away from the table, Hank thanked his wife and tipped her with a smile and what for him was a rave review. Every bit as good as Nora's, he told her. Hearing the dead woman's name took a little shine off the moment, but Marjorie was philosophical. Rome wasn't built in a day, she reassured herself. Soon enough, he'll stop the comparisons.

Marjorie hummed as she cleared away the dishes. She was pleased with herself. A cook is only as good as her recipes, Marjorie thought. And now she had Nora's prized recipes. It was a thought that kept her happily amused as she cleaned the kitchen.

The last item on the table was a large, white, ceramic platter, covered with grease and bits of ground meat. It was too awkward to fit in the dishwasher, so Marjorie washed the platter by hand. As

A slim notebook like this one, but older, held all of Nora's culinary secrets. Although the woman was dead, however, she seemed reluctant to let it go.

she rinsed away the soap under the running faucet, her heart nearly stopped. There, in the glossy finish of the dish, a face stared out at her. It was not the reflection of her own face—it was Nora. Marjorie recognized the roller-set hair, the eyeglasses and the features. The expression on Nora's face was nothing like the pleased one she wore in so many family portraits around the house, however. This Nora was scowling, seething, and had her eyes focused hatefully upon Marjorie. When the woman's ghostly image opened her mouth as if to speak, Marjorie shrieked. The soapy ceramic platter slipped from her hands, and crashed into the stainless steel sink.

It took several minutes for Marjorie to regain her composure. When she did, she chastised herself for her foolishness and quickly cleared away the ceramic shards of evidence. I have Nora on the brain, she thought, and resolved not to look at the book again that evening. But when night fell, Marjorie found herself dreaming about it.

In the dream, she had the little notebook clutched tightly to her chest as she ran through the house. Nora was chasing her—she knew it was Nora, although every time Marjorie glanced back over her shoulder, she could see no more than a shadow, a shifting shape or a column of shimmering air. At one point, she stopped running long enough to catch her ragged breath, and concealed herself behind the pantry door. As the kitchen clock ticked out agonizing seconds, Marjorie happened to glance down at the book in her hands. There were dark red stains blooming over the cabbage roses, now. Marjorie recoiled in disgust, the notebook dropped and somewhere Nora laughed. There was an icy breath of air on Marjorie's neck, and she felt herself try to scream...

The window was open. A cool night rain had begun to fall, and the breeze coming through the window was frigid. Marjorie sat up in bed, shaking with relief. She had been uncomfortably cold, and that had caused the nightmare. Nothing more dramatic than that. Still, after she shut the window, she scrambled back under the safety of the covers, ignoring the nagging call from her bladder. It was an hour before she felt brave enough to walk across the hall to her own bathroom.

A few days later, Marjorie's memory of the nightmare and the broken platter had faded, and she served Hank a delicious supper of Nora's Chicken Pot Pie and Summer Garden Salad. Again, the man seemed pleased, which in turn pleased Marjorie. At 3 AM the following morning, however, Hank's happy stomach hardly seemed worth it: Marjorie awakened to see a swirling white mist coalesce into a dense, human-shaped figure just outside the bedroom door.

At that moment, Marjorie accepted that she was not hallucinating. These things were not her imagination. She may have felt haunted by Nora before, but now she truly was haunted by Nora, and it was all because of the book—the damned little homemade cookbook, with its recipes for "Lazy Day Cake" and "Browned Peach Custard," that had defined Nora's reputation as a cook. As the shimmering white shape in the hall began to fade, Marjorie resolved to put the notebook back where it belonged.

In the morning, she had a single moment of weakness. As she sat on the foot of the bed and pulled the book out of the drawer from beneath its camouflage of clutter, she thought that it would be nice to make a special dessert for the next day's Sunday lunch. Hank's children would be coming by, and it would impress them to have Marjorie make a treat that was every bit as good as their mother's. As she mulled this over, Marjorie happened to glance up at the mirror above the bureau.

Nora's hate-filled face stared back at her.

The image lasted only a second, but it was long enough. Marjorie closed the book with a snap and marched down the stairs. She yanked open the door to the storage cupboard and pulled back the flap on one of the cardboard boxes. Without a second look, she tucked Nora's notebook inside and folded the box top back up. For good measure, she found a roll of packing tape in the utility room and sealed the carton tightly. It's all yours, Nora, she thought to herself, and noted that she felt much better as she went back up to the kitchen.

Hank usually spent his Saturday afternoons puttering around the house. While he fixed a leaky faucet in the kitchen, Marjorie sat at the table and flipped through a magazine. After an extended period of companionable silence, Hank asked what they might be having for supper. Marjorie looked up from her reading and told him.

"I thought we might just have sandwiches," she said. "I thought that if I didn't have to cook, then, when you're done there, we'd have time to go for a bit of a walk."

There was a pause as Hank gathered up his tools. Marjorie waited for the inevitable negative comment. But it never came.

Hank simply said that that sounded nice. After a moment, he added that Nora had never had time for anything like an afternoon walk. She had always been too busy in the kitchen.

Marjorie smiled, and, for the first time in her marriage to Hank, felt right at home.

Phantom Post

Sandra, who grew up in Kindersley during the 1970s, enjoyed a particularly close relationship with her aunt. The two lived hundreds of miles apart, but that never kept them from being in close communication.

"I probably wrote two or three letters a week to Auntie Bev," recalled Sandra. "I'd just tell her about all of my teenage problems—really pour my heart out. She always wrote back and she always had good advice for me. It was easier, you know, than going to my parents a lot of the time."

Sandra's aunt must have enjoyed being the young girl's confidante, for she always encouraged the correspondence. Christmas and birthday gifts usually consisted of pretty patterned or scented stationery, coloured pens, and pre-printed address labels. "There were always stamps, too," said Sandra. So there was never anything that kept the teen from writing.

Ironically, the woman who had advised Sandra through so many of life's little problems was to be the source of her greatest sorrow. When Sandra was 16, her Aunt Bev was killed in a car accident. Every member of the family grieved, but Sandra may have been the most affected by the tragedy on a daily basis.

"Every day, I'd find myself thinking, oh, I have to ask Auntie Bev about this or that," remembered Sandra. "I'd want her opinion, or her advice. Sometimes I just wanted to tell her something, like, 'I got a good grade,' or 'some boy was flirting with me.' Then I'd remember that she wasn't there to write to anymore."

Writing letters to Bev had been Sandra's bedtime ritual. After the woman's death, Sandra simply went to bed earlier, and often cried herself to sleep.

After several weeks, Sandra's parents became concerned that their normally lively daughter was not recovering from her loss. She had dark shadows haunting her eyes, and her grades had dropped. A teacher from one of Sandra's favourite classes had called to say that the girl seemed unenthusiastic and indecisive. Her level of energy and confidence seemed low. It was suggested that the girl might need some professional counselling. When Sandra's parents gently approached the subject with her, however, they met with total resistance.

"I just flatly refused," she later said. "At the time, I wasn't sure why, but later I kind of figured it out. Auntie Bev had been my counsellor, and I didn't want to replace her. Not so fast, anyway."

As Sandra got ready for bed that evening, she felt more downhearted than ever. Inside, she knew that she did need to speak to someone. But she honestly didn't know if she could share her turbulent emotions with anyone other than her trusted aunt. Sandra was thinking that the situation was hopeless, and she sighed deeply as she leaned over to turn off the bedside lamp.

Before her fingers touched the switch, she noticed something.

Just opposite the bed, in Sandra's small room, was her little writing desk. It was where she had always kept her stationery and pens. After Bev's death, however, she had cleaned off the surface, stashing every item that reminded her of letter writing deep in the desk's single drawer. But on that particular night, the desktop was not clear. Three items sat there, very deliberately positioned. There was an envelope, three sheets of paper and a lavender-coloured pen.

"I couldn't figure it out," said Sandra. "Not only were those things taken out of my drawer, but they were also taken out of the stationery box that they had been packed in. I didn't think my Mom would have done it. She was pretty good about respecting my privacy. So it was strange. I just sat there, on the edge of the bed, looking at this stuff for the longest time."

After several minutes, Sandra was overcome with a tremendous urge to write a letter to her aunt. She thought about how good it would feel to unburden herself on paper, knowing the words would reach a sympathetic reader. Then, immediately on the heels of that thought, she found herself thinking, well, why not?

The girl sat down at her desk and gingerly picked up the writing pen. It had been a gift from her aunt the previous Christmas. She ran her fingers lightly over the creamy sheets of stationery with their tiny cluster of painted pansies at the top. Also a gift from Aunt Bev. Sandra, who had anticipated that any reminder of her beloved aunt would only be painful, was surprised to find that there was comfort in these things. She picked up the pen, and wrote "Dear Auntie Bev."

"After that, the words just poured out," said Sandra. "I filled those three sheets, back and front with everything that I'd been feeling over the weeks. When those pages were full, I was going to get some more paper. But then it occurred to me that three pages were laid out, so maybe three pages were all I was supposed to write. I folded them up and put them in the envelope. I didn't know how I should address it, and there were no stamps on the desk, so I just wrote 'Auntie Bev' on the front. Then I hid it away on the top shelf of my closet and went back to bed."

Sandra remembers having a deep, dreamless and restful sleep that night. In the morning, she woke feeling better than she had in many weeks.

For months afterward, Sandra wrote letters to her aunt. The stationery was never set out on the desk for her again, but that didn't matter. The idea had been planted and had taken root. The teen sometimes wrote as many as three letters in a week, but they were never more than three pages in length. Always, when she finished, she would stash them away on the top shelf in her closet.

"That writing was just really therapeutic for me," Sandra said. "After a while, I really did start to feel better. My parents stopped trying to get me into counselling. And then, eventually, I found I wasn't writing as often. Then I got to the point where I didn't have to write to Auntie Bev at all anymore."

The question remains: did Sandra benefit solely from sorting out her feelings on paper, or was there a bit of supernatural help involved?

"I can only tell you three things," Sandra stated. "Number one: I don't know who set out the stationery for me on that first night. Number two: I always felt extremely close to Auntie Bev when I was writing to her. I mean, *extremely* close. And number three: when I went away to college a few years later, I couldn't find any of the letters that I had written. I know where I put them, and I'm sure that I never threw them away, but they just weren't there in the closet anymore."

Perhaps the letters were delivered after all, to a woman who managed to comfort her grieving niece all the way from the other side.

Photo of a Phantom

A man from Swift Current named Gary never believed in ghosts, until 1994. That was the year he was given an old family photo album, filled with images of relatives he knew and several he had never met. There was one, however, whom he was about to meet.

When Gary first received the album from an elderly aunt, he spent several hours flipping through its dry, yellow pages. He had a great interest in photography and examined each picture with care, wondering if the creases and scratches could be repaired. One portrait in particular seemed to demand his attention, although Gary could not see why. It showed a distant relative whom he had never known, posing proudly in front of a leafy hedge. The man wore a dapper, 1920s-era suit with a jaunty straw hat. Beneath the brim his dark eyes twinkled, and under a formidable mustache the man's mouth was turned up in a merry expression. The photo had no stains or damage, and Gary could not understand why he kept returning to it. Eventually, he decided that he simply found the picture appealing and put the album away without another thought.

That night, Gary found himself dreaming about the photo album with its crackling pages of black and white history. Around 3 AM he awoke with the image of the dream fresh in his memory. He rose to use the bathroom, and stood at the sink for several seconds while he had a drink of water. When he set the glass down, he glanced into the darkened mirror for no more than a moment, and was shocked at what he saw. There, superimposed over his own face, was the jovial visage of the man whose portrait Gary had found so intriguing. Gary gasped in shock and stumbled backward a step. In that instant, the image vanished.

A Swift Current man once received a family photo album that truly brought the past to life.

This is a waking dream, Gary thought to himself with a sense of wonder. He stepped forward and gazed more intently into the mirror, but could not re-create the hallucination. Wondering once more why the mustached man held such appeal for him, Gary returned to bed and went back to sleep. He dreamed no more of the photo album that night.

Several nights later, Gary was sleeping once again when a sudden chill awoke him. Thinking that his wife had rolled over and taken the covers with her, Gary began sleepily to grope for the blankets. He found himself as well tucked in as ever. Confused, Gary opened his eyes and saw the source of the icy cold air.

It was the man from the photo, standing beside his bed, staring down at him.

Gary was too stunned to move. He simply stared at the apparition, who stared back at him, seemingly amused. After a moment, Gary realized that he had been holding his breath, and exhaled in a jagged stream. The air that left his mouth immediately condensed into white vapor. At the sight of this, the ghost's head bobbed slightly as if in a suppressed snort of laughter. He winked at Gary and vanished. The bedroom air began to warm, almost immediately.

The next day, Gary said nothing to his family of his mysterious nocturnal guest. After dinner had been cleared away that evening, however, he pulled out the old album. Carefully, he laid it out on the kitchen table and turned to the page he had looked at so often. There was no doubt. It was the same man. Gary resolved to speak to his aunt and find out who the fellow was. He wasn't convinced yet that he believed in spirits, but there was something going on that he couldn't explain.

As Gary was about to put the photos away, his four-year-old daughter climbed up on his lap. She pored over the pages with great interest, and became particularly excited when she saw the portrait of the genial gentleman by the hedge. "I know that man!" she exclaimed. "He comes to visit, sometimes! That's Uncle Mo!"

Gary placed a phone call to his office the next morning and explained that he wouldn't be in. He then wrapped the photo album carefully and put it on the front passenger seat of his car. It kept him company as he made the two-hour drive to his aunt's home. When he got there, he showed the elderly woman the photo and asked her to identify the man. She adjusted her glasses and looked carefully at the face.

"Oh, that would be Morris," she said. "He was Ruth's brother, so that would make him your great-uncle, I suspect." She then turned her attention to Gary, and inquired, "Why do you ask?"

"No reason," he replied.

Gary never told his aunt the truth and never mentioned the strange incidents to anyone else. But from that point on, he was more open-minded regarding the paranormal. After all, he knew from experience that sometimes relatives can return.

The Rocking Chair Baby

A woman named Cathy who lives in Melfort, Saskatchewan, had only one regret when she was expecting her first child.

"I wished that my mother could have been there to share the experience with me," she said. "My husband and I had been trying to get pregnant for a long time, and before we did manage to conceive, Mom passed away. So, as happy as I was about the baby, there was this little sad part of me that just wished she could have known about it."

Cathy consoled herself by taking a few things that had been left to her by her mother out of storage. Among the cherished items was a maple rocking chair, which was placed in the nursery. It seemed to Cathy to be a way of including her mother in preparations for the baby.

"It was nice to have it in there. When I was decorating the room, I'd often take a break and just rock in the chair for a while. I felt close to my Mom, and close to my baby. It was like we were all there together." Eventually, Cathy would come to suspect that her mother was there even when she and her unborn child were not.

One afternoon, as Cathy was walking down the hall past the nursery, she spotted some movement out of the corner of her eye. She backed up a step, glanced in the room and noticed that her mother's maple rocking chair was moving ever so slightly.

"The window was open a little, so I blamed it on that," she remembered. "There was no breeze that day, but it was the only logical explanation."

She didn't give the incident another thought until one evening, when her husband mentioned something to her.

"He said that we might want to level out the floor in the baby's room before replacing the carpet," said Cathy. "When I asked him why he thought so, he told me that it was obviously on a slant, because he'd seen the rocking chair move by itself." The next day, out of curiosity, Cathy took a level out of the household tool box and walked into the baby's room. She set the instrument on several different spots on the floor, including the place where the rocking chair normally sat. Every time, the bubbles lined up exactly even. There was nothing wrong with the floor in the room, and Cathy was starting to think that the rocking chair did have a mind of its own. Perhaps more accurately, she thought that her mother—who most definitely had a strong mind of her own—was still enjoying the use of her rocking chair.

"It was a strange feeling, but not a bad one," said Cathy. "In fact, it was comforting. I went into the nursery as often as ever and sat in that chair, and thought about my mother and my baby. When there was no one around to think that I was a lunatic, I would talk out loud to both of them."

As Cathy's pregnancy progressed and she spent more and more time relaxing in the nursery, the spiritual presence became more pronounced. One night, as she made a trip to the bathroom, she saw the rocker making more movement than ever before. Amazed, she watched the chair for several minutes as it moved back and forth. Eventually it slowed and came to a stop. Another night, she saw something in the room that appeared to be a faint mist. There was no colour or light to the form, but what she would later describe as "a sort of shimmering, or thickening of the air." Objects behind the shape seemed to be distorted. Again, the phenomenon lasted a minute or two and then vanished. Again, Cathy was awed but not the least bit frightened.

"I knew that whatever it was, it was not going to harm us. And, frankly, I had a really strong feeling that it was my mother." Cathy kept her "really strong feeling" to herself, however. Fearing that no one else would believe her or appreciate the significance of what was happening, she never shared her stories. Not even her husband knew.

Interestingly, the spiritual activity only lasted for a few months. After Cathy gave birth to a baby girl and brought her home, there were no more strange happenings in the nursery. The rocking chair remained still, and no mysterious, rippling shapes ever again appeared. Cathy felt an empty space in the room—something had vanished. Cathy began to feel she knew why, when her baby grew into a chubby toddler .

"My daughter looks a lot like my Mom," she said, when the girl was three years old. "I've never been too sure if I believe in reincarnation, but you never know. It would be nice if it was true."

There's no way of knowing if Cathy's daughter is the reincarnated spirit of her mother. What does seem certain is this: for a few months, the spirit of Cathy's mother was present, and the two shared a very special time in the younger woman's life.

Uncle Richard's Return

In the early 1940s, an eleven-year-old boy named Karl was living a happy and rather carefree life on his parents' farm in southern Saskatchewan. His days were filled with schoolwork, chores and friends. Best of all, Karl's grandparents lived on a neighbouring farm, along with their youngest son, Richard.

Karl's Uncle Richard was in his late teens, but still seemed to enjoy spending time with the younger boy. He would show him the best spots for fishing in the creek, and the best way to catch grasshoppers in a jar. Richard taught Karl to whistle, skate and slide into home plate. Two or three times a week, the teenager would walk the three miles to visit his nephew, always following the path of the railway tracks that ran between the two farms. If Karl knew when his uncle would be coming, he'd walk along the tracks in the opposite direction to meet him. As soon as the two caught sight of each other, they'd raise their hands high in a greeting.

Karl's parents would often listen to the radio in the evenings to hear news of the war in Europe. His teacher spent some time at the beginning of each day pointing out places on the big map, where important battles were being fought. Still, the reality of the situation never hit home for Karl until his Uncle Richard joined up and was sent overseas to fight. To the younger boy, who had never been farther away than Regina, it sounded like a terrifically exciting adventure. He was wise enough to keep that opinion to himself, though—especially around his grandmother, whose lips were set in a tight line for weeks after Richard left.

Months passed, and Karl sorely missed his uncle's companion-ship. He paid more attention now when the old Hudson's Bay Company radio was switched on after supper, and he looked forward to the days when the family received letters from overseas. Once there was even a letter addressed specifically to Karl. In large, loopy script, Richard told the boy about the strange country he was in and the new things he was experiencing. He wrote down a word in a foreign language, and then explained afterward that it meant "hello." At the end of the letter, he promised that when he came home, he and Karl would put a map of Europe on the wall and use pins to mark all the places he had been. Karl read the letter several times and then tucked it away safely in a drawer. It was days before he realized that Uncle Richard hadn't actually written a word about the war itself.

During the summer of 1944, Karl turned twelve. It was a milestone he wished he could have shared with his favourite uncle, but Richard was still off fighting in the war. Karl didn't even know exactly where his uncle's company was—there hadn't been a letter in some time. The lack of communication seemed to make the family nervous, although no one talked about it in front of the children. Once, Karl had overheard his mother reassuring his grandmother. "It's a war," he heard her say, "and the mail doesn't move like regular." Karl tried to remember that himself. Although nobody realized it, he was old enough to worry, too.

One sweltering afternoon when chores were done and the sky was a perfect, cloudless blue, Karl decided to take a walk. The boy had no particular destination in mind, but ended up following the railway tracks toward his grandparents' farm. The air above the steel rods shimmered in the afternoon heat. The occasional lazy insect hummed near Karl's perspiring, sunburned skin and was swatted away. It was peaceful and still, and Karl felt very alone in the world. But then he spotted some movement in the distance.

The spirit of a young man who died in the Second World War returned once to the familiar railway tracks near his home. His purpose was to bid farewell to a favourite nephew.

Karl squinted at the horizon, wondering who or what was moving along the tracks toward him. He laid a hand on the rails and felt no vibration, and there wasn't the faintest noise, so it couldn't be a train. The boy wondered if it was an animal, and if he shouldn't perhaps be turning back home. While Karl considered what to do, he kept walking forward, and the distance between him and the approaching shape closed. Suddenly, Karl realized that it was a man walking along the tracks. In the same moment that he realized this, the man raised his arm in what was to Karl a very familiar greeting. The boy felt his stomach lurch with excitement.

Walking was suddenly not fast enough. Karl broke into a run, mindless of the afternoon heat and the perspiration that rolled down his neck and back. His shoes pounded out a steady rhythm on the wooden ties and spit bits of gravel out behind him. The man (who could only be Uncle Richard, Karl had decided) continued to walk at the same, steady pace, but it was obvious why. Despite the high temperature, he wore a full soldier's uniform, including heavy boots and a helmet. He carried a heavy pack of gear and a rifle. Uncle Richard's home, thought Karl, and he's going to show me all his war stuff.

The boy ran until his lungs and head felt ready to explode with the heat. Gasping in hot breath, he slowed to a walk and wiped the sweat from his face. The soldier was closer now, and as he raised his head and looked directly at Karl, the boy was overjoyed. It *was* Uncle Richard! It was definitely him. Thinking of how happy and relieved his parents were going to be was a treat sweeter than candy.

Uncle Richard did look tired though. He walked with his shoulders slumped and it seemed to take a great effort for him to put one foot in front of the other. Karl realized that he would be needing a good, long rest, and saw no reason why it couldn't start immediately.

"Uncle Richard!" he shouted. "Sit down and rest for a bit! I'll be right there to help you carry your stuff!"

Richard stopped walking, and looked up at his nephew. He was close enough now for Karl to see the dark pockets under his eyes and the mud smeared on his face and clothing. The boy could see none of his uncle's former energy when Richard raised his arm once more in the salute they had so often shared. When his arm dropped wearily back to his side, Richard suddenly somehow seemed as insubstantial as the heat waves above the railway tracks. Karl would remember forever that one moment, he was looking at Uncle Richard, and that the next moment, he seemed able to look *through* him, and the moment after that, he was gone.

The boy felt a wave of nausea, and sat down hard on the ground. The sun still beat down, the air remained still and the bugs chirped and buzzed as though nothing had happened. It was quite some time before Karl felt capable of walking home. When he finally did, he went directly into the house and told his mother that he had had too much sun. The woman took one look at her son's hectic appearance and agreed. Karl spent the rest of the afternoon in his darkened bedroom with a cool cloth over his eyes. The damp flannel felt refreshing, but did nothing to block out the image that had been burned into Karl's mind: it was the image of Uncle Richard, weak and worn, raising his arm in one final, friendly salute.

Days later, Karl's grandparents received the telegram. Richard had died in battle. It had happened on the day that Karl met him on the tracks.

The family grieved, and eventually healed. Karl grew older and dealt with his loss by learning as much as he could about the war. By himself, he hung a map of Europe on his bedroom wall, and pinpointed the places his uncle was likely to have been.

Years after his strange experience, when Karl was older than Richard ever got to be, he came across the letter that his uncle had sent him. The foreign word that had been unrecognizable to Karl as a boy was now obvious and easy. It was "bonjour." Richard had been in France when he wrote to his nephew. It was a small discovery, but one that allowed Karl to feel closer to his uncle than he had since the last day he saw him—the day the young man had died, and had come home to wave farewell by the railway tracks.

Grandfather's Presence

A woman named Marylee Lester grew up in southeastern Saskatchewan, but spent a great deal of time on her grandmother's farm, five miles east of Kerrobert. The white farmhouse built by her grandparents was a gathering place for the extended family. Marylee and her brother, Peter, spent all of the major holidays and some of every summer vacation there. Today, they have many stories to share about those times—including some of a decidedly ghostly nature.

"I was too young to know my granddad, since I was about two years old when he passed away," recalled Marylee. "However, every once in a while, out of the corner of my eye, I would see a silhouette of the profile of a man sitting in a chair. When I went to look straight at it, it always disappeared. For a while, I didn't say anything, but once I determined that it wasn't my mind playing tricks on me, I told my brother about what I saw. What I didn't realize was that he had [been seeing] the same thing I had, all along!"

Marylee and Peter decided to tell their grandmother about the shadowy sightings. The woman said that she had never noticed anything of the kind herself, but did confirm that the old recliner where the image always appeared had been her husband's favourite chair.

One New Year's Eve years later, Marylee had a different but equally mysterious experience in the house.

"I saw someone go into the kitchen," she said. "It was so real, I followed, thinking it was Peter. When I got into the kitchen, there was no one there. So I went into the [adjoining] pantry. Again, there was no one. Assuming Peter was planning a scare for me, I said, 'I know you're in there.' But just then I heard his voice, along with everyone else's, *upstairs*. I went to tell him what had just happened, [but before I could] he said that I looked like I had just seen a ghost!

"The next day, when we were discussing this, a Christmas ornament that was hanging on the wall above me suddenly came off and fell."

Peter experienced other phenomena, as well. On one occasion, he was in one of the upstairs bedrooms, which simply had curtains for doors. He saw a shadow pass by in the hall and called out to his mother to bring him a glass of water when she returned from downstairs. When his mother answered, "What?" Peter could hear that she was still in her own bedroom. At that point he also realized that there had been no creaking of the floorboards or stairs, which always sounded loudly whenever anyone walked upon them.

Marylee recalls that a much younger cousin would sometimes refuse to go upstairs because of "the strange man up there," but believes that no one else saw the apparition of who she believes was her grandfather. Her conclusion? "It seemed that he was just checking up on the grandchildren that he never got to know."

When Marylee eventually told her father about the visitations, she learned that her grandfather may not have been the only spirit on the premises. "My dad told me that both he and his brother saw a disembodied horse's head float by the window once when they were young. Of course, this was while my granddad was still alive, so I guess the house was always haunted in one way or another."

That house has been standing vacant for some time. Although the farm remains in the hands of relatives, Marylee hasn't visited recently.

"I haven't been in that house… since my grandmother passed away," she said. "I just hope that [my grandparents] have found each other now, and have gone to their final resting place together."

Chances are that they have, secure in their knowledge that the grandkids are doing just fine.

Hide and Shriek

A man named Lowell spent most of the summers of his childhood on his grandparents' farm, south of Regina. Lowell's parents found that sending their three children to the farm was an excellent alternative to pricey child care in the city, as well as a chance for the kids to stretch their legs, breathe country air and bond with the only grandmother and grandfather that they had. Lowell and his brother and sister had a different point of view, however. They found the summers unbearably long. They were separated from their parents and friends, trapped in what they felt was a hopelessly dull environment, and forced to live with the rules and company of an elderly couple with whom they never forged a close or loving relationship. The days and weeks seemed unbearably long, and Lowell in particular retained few fond memories of those times.

"At best, it was just incredibly boring," he recalled. "At worst, it could be pretty unpleasant. My grandfather would get it into his head that we were disrespectful, or lazy, or whatever, and we'd be lined up against the kitchen wall. We'd have to face the wall, and keep our noses touching it, and keep perfectly still until he thought we'd learned whatever lesson this was supposed to teach us. Grandma wasn't much better, but mostly she just ignored us unless we had to be corrected over our manners or the way we did our chores."

The three children tried to stay out of the house and out of the way as much as possible. They played in the barn and other out-buildings when the weather was fine, and in the dark, damp basement of the house when it was raining. It was during such a cold, rainy day in the summer of 1972 that Lowell had an experience that he has neither forgotten nor been able to explain to this day. It began with a simple game that the children played in the basement. "The basement of that old house was pretty gross," said Lowell, "almost more of a cellar. It was used for storage, so it was all shelves and boxes with a few closets built against the wall where my grandmother would keep her canned preserves. Nothing was ever cleaned down there, so we'd just get filthy with dust when we played. That meant catching hell once—but it was better than try-ing to play upstairs, where we'd get ragged on all day long. Anyway, because it was so cluttered and filled with junk, it meant that there were a lot of places to hide."

Because of that, hide-and-seek was usually the activity of choice in the basement. On the particular day that Lowell remem-bers, he was on a lucky streak. He had found so many effective hiding places that he hadn't once been tagged "it." The kids were playing their fourth round of the game when he discovered what he thought to be the best spot of all.

"It was like a big, old pantry cupboard that had been pushed into one corner. It had shelves in it that went about two-thirds of the way down, but the bottom part was just one big space. I was only nine years old, and I wasn't that big, so I could squeeze into the bottom of the cupboard and pull the doors shut with my fin-gernails. It was absolutely pitch black in there, and like an oven, but I knew my brother and sister would never find me."

Lowell also discovered that when he was inside the antique cupboard, he couldn't hear very well what was taking place outside the heavy wooden doors. He would simply have to make sure that the others had had ample time to give up before he revealed his hideout. For several minutes, he waited patiently, giving his sister, who was "it," plenty of time to find his younger brother. The muscles in his legs cramped in objection to their uncomfortable position. Lowell shifted his aching limbs, one at a time, making use of the few spare inches he had. Trickling lines of sweat began to course down his neck and back. Something—likely a spider—made its feathery way up his leg. Still, Lowell remained determinedly quiet, waiting for enough time to pass.

"Finally, I figured it was long enough. They must have given up. So I went to push the doors open, but they wouldn't move."

Lowell leaned into the heavy wooden panels with his thin shoulder, but to no avail. He tried to twist around so he could kick at the doors with his feet, but there simply wasn't enough room. It occurred to the boy that if he couldn't hear much of what was going on outside the cupboard, perhaps anyone who was outside couldn't hear him. With that thought, panic began to take root. Lowell hammered helplessly on the doors with his fists, screaming for his siblings to save him.

"I was yelling at the top of my lungs," remembered Lowell, "and inside the cupboard, it was echoing, so it seemed even louder. And that's why what happened next immediately seemed unreal."

What happened was that someone spoke. It was a man's voice—low and even, nearly a whisper, yet Lowell heard it so clearly over his own clamour that he often wondered later if it had been inside his head. At the time, it seemed to come directly from the other side of the doors. "You're trapped!" the voice announced with quiet glee. "Let's see how you like hiding now!"

"At that point, I just flipped," said Lowell. "I was yelling my head off, and bouncing my fists off every surface, and kicking… you name it. I was even bashing my head against the doors, and I remember seeing these little flashes of light behind my eyes. I think I would have passed out in a minute or two, but then the doors opened."

There was a rush of cool air from outside the cupboard, and Lowell fell out of the cubby hole onto the rough, dirty concrete floor. He lay panting and crying at the feet of his brother and sister, who stood over him wearing expressions of confusion. Finally, when Lowell had calmed himself a bit, they dared to ask some questions.

"How did you get in there?" asked his sister. Lowell told her that he had just climbed in and closed the doors behind him.

"No, we mean how did you pull the trunk in front of the doors after you were inside?" she said.

"I didn't know what she was talking about," Lowell later explained. "I mean, how could I have barricaded the doors after I climbed in? But I looked over at my little brother, and he was sitting on this huge, old trunk that my grandparents owned. And then I looked at the floor, and I could see a trail cut through all the dust and garbage, where they had pulled this thing away from the cupboard. Someone had trapped me in there, and I know to this day that it wasn't my brother or sister. And if anyone else had been there, those guys would have seen them."

At that time, however, figuring out the identity of the culprit did not seem as urgent as did the need to get out of the basement. All three children quickly made their way upstairs, where they received the expected tongue-lashing for soiling their clothes, and were ordered to wash themselves thoroughly before dinner. They said nothing to their grandparents, but from that day forward they stayed clear of the farmhouse basement on even the rainiest of days.

"You know, it wasn't until about 20 years later that I had any idea what might have happened," Lowell later said. "I was having a couple of drinks with my dad, and I was finally telling him how much we hated those summers at the farm. I was telling him about some of the brutal punishments Grandpa would hand out, and Dad said, 'Yeah, your grandfather was a tough old bird, but he was mild compared to *his* father.' And then Dad started telling me this story about one time when he hadn't done his chores. His grandfather was looking to hand out a beating, so Dad went down to the basement to hide. He said to me, 'I hid in the bottom of that old cupboard with all the shelves, you know the one I mean?' I found that my throat was suddenly too dry to speak, so I simply nodded. Then I listened with a growing sense of déjà vu as Dad went on to describe what had happened.

"He told me that his grandfather had followed him down to the basement, and saw him crawling into the cupboard. The old man figured it would be a good lesson for Dad if he was stuck in there for a little while, so he pushed something heavy up against the doors. Dad never knew exactly what it was, but I'm willing to bet it was the steamer trunk. I finally found my voice, and asked Dad, 'Did he say anything to you?' Dad nodded and said, 'He told me something like, "Let's see how you like hiding now." Then he left me in there for an hour. When I came out, I got a beating.' Dad then changed the topic, and the matter was unofficially closed forever. We never talked about it again," said Lowell, "but from then on I knew who had locked me in the cupboard."

Was it actually the ghost of Lowell's great-grandfather, or a supernatural replaying of events that had taken place decades earlier? The only certainty is this: it pays to be careful where you hide. There is no telling who or what might seek you out.

Chapter 5

CRIME AND PUNISHMENT

*Nothing stirs a spirit quite
as much as a sense of having
been done wrong.
Or is it that nothing makes one
quite so sensitive to paranormal
phenomena as a guilty conscience?
It is difficult to know. What is certain
is that crime (particularly murder)
often results in a haunting. Predictably,
the focus of the ghostly activity is
usually the guilty party.*

*It has often been said: "Don't do
the crime if you can't do the time."
And bear in mind that,
on some planes of existence,
a sentence may be eternal.*

The Mentalist and the Murder Case

It was December 10, 1932, and the little movie theatre in Beechy, Saskatchewan, was beginning to hum with life. Outside, ice crystals hung in the air and the sound of feet crunching over hard-packed snow could be heard as people approached the building. Inside, everyone chatted and laughed and was flushed with anticipation. It was not a movie they had come to see, nor a Christmas pageant, though there were a few cheerful hand-made decorations lending their festive appeal. This night, the people of the small community north of Swift Current had gathered to witness a live performance by a mind-reader who billed himself as "Professor Gladstone, Mentalist." The audience was hoping for a night of excitement and drama. They would not be disappointed.

The lights were dimmed and a hush fell over the auditorium. Professor Gladstone appeared on the stage. He was tall and grey-haired, with the distinguished appearance and dramatic flair necessary for one in his profession. For nearly an hour, the audience sat rapt as the travelling psychic astounded and amused them with his uncanny powers. Then, in the middle of his act, Professor Gladstone seemed to falter. For several long seconds, the man stopped performing. People began to shift uncomfortably in their seats, and a low murmur spread throughout the crowd. It stopped when Gladstone suddenly straightened and fixed his piercing gaze upon a local rancher named Bill Taylor.

"You are thinking of your friend Scotty McLauchlan," the mind reader boomed. "He was murdered. Brutally murdered."

The townspeople sat in shocked silence.

Scotty McLauchlan had been a popular fellow who once farmed in the area. Three years before Professor Gladstone brought his show to the small town, McLauchlan had been talking about leaving. He had plans to sell his share of the farm to his partner, John Schumacher, and then take the night train to British Columbia. On January 16, 1930, the planned evening of McLauchlan's departure, a number of friends gathered at the railway depot to bid him farewell. McLauchlan never arrived. His disappearance was a mystery that the RCMP was unable to solve, so the case was closed.

Apparently, however, Professor Gladstone did not believe in closed cases, for after his announcement regarding McLauchlan's murder, he pointed to another man in the audience with a dramatic flourish. "He will find the body!" Gladstone shouted. "And I shall be with him when he does!" The audience gasped in shock, for the man Gladstone had singled out was Beechy's off-duty RCMP officer, Constable Carey.

The audience certainly got their money's worth that night. Even Constable Carey was impressed enough with the mentalist to call police headquarters in Saskatoon the next morning. He spoke with Corporal Jack Woods, and relayed the events of the previous evening. Corporal Woods briefly checked into Professor Gladstone's reputation, and decided to travel to Beechy to reopen the case. After all, he told Constable Carey, they might as well take advantage of the sensation that the psychic's revelation had created. If people were once again talking about McLauchlan's disappearance, the RCMP would do well to listen.

The morning after Corporal Woods arrived in town, he and Constable Carey took Professor Gladstone on a tour of Beechy's farming community. One by one, they knocked at the rough-hewn doors of simple log shacks on snowbound homesteads. Throughout the day, they listened to the same useless speculation that they had heard nearly three years before. But late in the afternoon, when they were about to give up, something new came to light. A normally tight-lipped farmer who was impressed by Gladstone's abilities gave the two officers a new lead. He admitted that there had been one time when McLauchlan's partner, John Schumacher, had visited him while in a terrible rage. The farmer didn't know why Schumacher was angry, but said that he had, at one point, claimed he would someday kill the "damned Scotsman." Prompted by this new bit of information, the Mounties and the mind reader drove out to John Schumacher's farm that same night.

As the men drove into Schumacher's yard, Professor Gladstone's senses snapped to attention. "Scotty McLauchlan's body is around here somewhere," he said. "I know it." If John Schumacher also knew it, though, he was admitting nothing. He simply repeated the story he had told at the time of his partner's disappearance. Scotty McLauchlan had wanted to leave for British Columbia, he said. He had paid Scotty a few hundred dollars in cash for his share of the land. He had never seen Scotty again. He had no idea where he was.

Woods and Carey were suspicious, and began to ask John Schumacher more pointed questions. The farmer became stubbornly silent. There seemed to be a solid impasse, when suddenly Professor Gladstone spoke.

"I'll tell you what happened," the psychic said, excitedly. "Scotty went over to the barn. You followed him and started a quarrel. There was a fight and Scotty fell. You struck, and struck, and struck… then you buried his body near the barn."

John Schumacher blanched, but said nothing. His silence would not buy him much more time, however. A group of men arrived at his farm the next morning, along with the two RCMP officers and Professor Gladstone. They gathered near the barn and awaited Gladstone's instructions. The professor concentrated for a few moments, then directed the men to a pile of frozen manure. "Under there you'll find all that remains of Scotty," he said. The men took hold of their picks and shovels and began to dig.

Two hours later, hands were numb and the group was beginning to lose faith. Then suddenly one of the men unearthed a woolen sock. The excitement of the find re-energized the diggers, and soon an entire skeleton had been excavated. Shreds of rotting cloth clung to the bones. It was enough to solve the case.

"It's Scotty all right!" one man shouted. "I'd know that scarf and mackinaw anywhere!"

It was agreed that the clothing had belonged to Scotty McLauchlan. The skull dug up from beneath the manure pile showed three distinct fractures. John Schumacher was confronted with the new evidence and finally admitted his guilt. He had murdered his partner—and gotten away with it, until Professor Gladstone came to town.

John Schumacher was convicted and sentenced in a Kindersley courtroom, and the RCMP was able to close the case for good. As for Professor Gladstone, he enjoyed tremendous publicity following the case and performed on the stage for many years. However, he was never again able to duplicate the drama of his show at Beechy, that December night in 1932.

The Crawling Coat

In 1932, there were two sisters living in a small house on the outskirts of Regina. They both worked for the same employer, a pharmacist who owned a small drug store and confectionery. The sisters had very different personalities, however, and made very different employees. The younger girl, Harriet, was honest and trustworthy. The elder one, Moira, tended to be sneaky and selfish. Every day that she worked in the store, she took a little money for herself out of the cash drawer. Even worse, this forced Harriet, who never wanted to be a thief, to do the same thing. If she didn't, she was sure that the pharmacist would notice the glaring differences between their daily receipts and have Moira arrested. Harriet agonized over what she had to do to protect her sister, and refused to keep the money. Moira ended up with all of it, and suffered no guilt whatsoever.

For weeks the scam continued, until Moira became concerned about having so much cash hidden under her mattress. If anyone ever found her nest egg, it would be extremely difficult to explain. She looked around the little two-room shack and found a suitable "bank" for her booty. It was a lovely black wool coat that she and Harriet had pooled their earnings to buy. When the weather was cold, the girls took turns wearing it: it was an arrangement that generally worked very well, as they worked on alternate days. This was an extremely warm March day, however, and Harriet had gone off to work wearing only a sweater. Moira thought it would be ideal to hide her fortune in the lining of the garment. Delighted with the idea, she found a pair of scissors and began to snip away at the stitches.

By the time Harriet arrived home that evening, Moira had finished the task and carefully sewed the lining back into the coat.

She said nothing to Harriet, thinking that it would be better if her highly moral little sister remained ignorant about what she was wearing on her back.

The next day, it was Moira's turn to work at the store. The mercurial March weather had turned cold again overnight, so she took the black coat down from it's usual peg by the door. As Moira slipped it on over her shoulders, she noted that it had a slightly different feel. The bills are just a little crisp, she thought. They'll soften up with time. She felt fairly certain that Harriet, who knew nothing of the impromptu alteration, would not notice the subtle difference.

By the time Moira had arrived at the confectionery, however, she was no longer sure that the difference was so subtle. Several times she had had to tug the coat down over her hips, because the fabric seemed to be riding up her body. And she was positive that the collar was now sitting differently. Something about it made the hair on the back of her neck stand up with static electricity. Even the sleeves, which had been perfect before, wanted to bunch up oddly around Moira's elbows. At the store, she was happy to take the uncomfortable coat off, but was worried about what Harriet would think the next time she wore it. Moira mulled the problem over throughout the work day. By closing time, she had a solution.

Believing that it was best to deal with the problem offensively, Moira assumed a pouty expression before walking into the little house that night. "Did you have this coat cleaned?" she asked Harriet, accusingly. Harriet shook her head, no. "Well, there's something wrong with it. Maybe the damp has ruined it, but it just doesn't feel comfortable, anymore." Moira flung the coat onto its peg and walked off to the bedroom in a dramatic huff, certain that she had handled any potential problems. Now, when Harriet put the coat on, she wouldn't be surprised by the odd fit.

What surprised Moira the next day was that Harriet didn't

notice any difference in the garment. "I can't think of what you mean, about it bunching up," the younger sister shrugged, then added gently, "Perhaps you've just put on a pound or two, Mo." Moira simply sniffed. Later, she realized that she should be pleased that Harriet was so sure the coat was fine. Somehow, the whole thing bothered her, however. It bothered her enough that, late that night when her sister was fast asleep, Moira tiptoed out of the bedroom and tried the coat on over her nightgown.

It made her flesh crawl.

When she had last worn it, she had been rushing to work, and was unable to discern her own movement from that of the cloth. Now, as she stood still in the darkened room, she could feel the coat writhing ever so slightly on her body. Repulsed, she shrugged it off and let it fall on the floor. Without bothering to hang the coat up on the wall again, she went back to bed. I'm either crazy or having a nightmare, she thought.

In the morning, when watery spring sunshine filtered through the thin curtains and woke her, Moira decided that the nightmare explanation made most sense. The coat may have become ill-fitting, but it certainly couldn't have taken on a life of its own.

Moira held this opinion for about five seconds, until she swung her feet out of bed and placed them on the floor. They landed on wool.

As Moira recoiled in disgust, she knew that she had not experienced a nightmare. She really had tried the coat on during the night and felt it moving slyly over her skin. She really had dropped it on the floor by the front door, and now she knew that, while she slept, it had been creeping ever closer to her. She dared not wonder what might have happened had she slept an hour longer.

There was a hairbrush sitting on the bedside table, and Moira used it to pick the coat up gingerly from the floor. Holding it out at arm's length, she proceeded carefully into the other room and deposited the foul thing on a hook. Satisfied that it would not be able to squirm down from its perch, Moira felt secure enough to turn her back on it while she got ready for work.

As she was stoking a fire to warm the little rooms, Harriet came out of the bedroom, yawning. "I'm glad I caught you before you left," she said to Moira. "There was something I needed to tell you last night." Harriet then went on to warn Moira that she would have to stop skimming the cash box at the confectionery. The pharmacist was changing his method of bookkeeping, and would now be sure to notice if the revenue and the inventory didn't match up. "It's for the best," Harriet lectured. "You shouldn't have been taking it, anyway."

Moira, who was too preoccupied to argue, just nodded mutely. She thought it too bad that her supplemental income had come to an end, but consoled herself with the knowledge that she at least had her savings. It appeared that her method of storing the money would have to change, but at least it was there. It was a comfort.

A few minutes later, Moira put on a faded, old coat and prepared to leave for work. "You'll be cold in that," advised Harriet. "Take the black wool." Moira mumbled that it just didn't suit her anymore and she'd prefer to be blue with the cold than to wear something so ill-fitting. In an obviously black mood, she left, slamming the door behind her.

All that day, as Moira traded licorice whips for pennies and listened to old ladies complain about the fact that you couldn't buy a good health tonic anymore, she worked on her problem. It was obvious, she thought, that the money must be taken out of the coat's silky lining. She would find another place to keep her stash—perhaps under a floorboard, or beneath the heavy trunk which was never moved. Then with any luck the coat would go back to just being a coat, and not some grotesque thing that felt like a swarm of insects on her skin. Moira shuddered to think of it, and looked forward to accomplishing her task on the next warm day when Harriet would leave the house without wearing the coat.

That evening, she returned home to find Harriet waiting for her. The younger sister was beaming with pleasure over something, and had even prepared a little bit of supper for the two of them. "I have a surprise for you, Mo," she said, and invited Moira to take her seat at the chipped, kitchen table. "Wait here."

With that, Harriet raced off into the other room. In a moment, she was back, and modelling a lovely, stylish, tan coat. There were tortoiseshell buttons decorating the pockets and a smart little faux fur trim at the collar.

"That's beautiful," Moira said, sincerely. "But it's not like you to spend your money on clothes."

"Well, it's for you!" Harriet spoke excitedly, then explained, "For us, that is. I thought we could share it. You just seem to dislike the black coat so much now, and I wanted to do something nice for you. So here we are! I even bought it just a little roomier than the other," she finished discretely, then shrugged the coat off her shoulders and offered it to Moira to try on.

Moira rose from the table and took the lovely wrap in her hands. It was beautiful, and looked so warm. She slipped it on over her drab uniform, and stepped back to view herself in the mirror. I look marvelous, she thought. Harriet chattered away happily behind her, apparently expressing that very opinion. Moira turned and preened in the mirror for several minutes, then suddenly was hit with a thought.

"How did you pay for this?" she demanded of Harriet. The girl looked pleased that she had asked.

"Moira, that's the best part!" she said. "It didn't cost a dime. I just took the black wool to that second-hand clothing store downtown and made a trade! The clerk was so happy, because there was a woman shopping in the store who bought our old coat straight away! Isn't that great!"

Moira heard herself faintly saying, "Yes, great," as she felt the colour drain from her cheeks. Once more, she looked in the mirror. It was a beautiful coat that she was wearing, but it couldn't hide the stoop in her posture or the bitterness in her eyes. It was a gorgeous coat, thought Moira, and unlikely to make the hair on her arms stand up in revulsion. But somehow, that wasn't enough. If she wore this coat for the next 40 years, it would never be worth what she had paid for it.

In the lining of the black wool had been over $200.

Greed, Revenge and *Murder*!

In a province known for its shimmering lakes, there is one that will always stand out to a woman named Margo. She knows it as Lake Qu'Appelle, and it is a peaceful spot only a short distance from Margo's Regina home. It is not the lake's proximity, nor its relaxing atmosphere that makes Qu'Appelle's waters notable to Margo, however. It is a frightening tale, told to her by her grandmother more than 50 years ago.

"My grandma used to tell me some fantastic stories," said Margo. "I don't know if a single one of them was true, but she told them with complete conviction and I was totally captivated every time. One of my favourites was this really spooky story that took place at Lake Qu'Appelle. She always began by saying, 'This is a tale of greed, revenge, and *murder!*' I knew the story off by heart, but I'd still jump halfway out of my seat every time she said that."

According to Margo's storytelling grandmother, there was once a couple who lived in a little house overlooking the blue waters of the lake. The wife was a hard worker, who had managed to put aside quite a bit of money, but the husband was a lazy sort who had a roving eye.

The wife went away to visit her sister for a week, and by day four the husband had another woman in his bed. The girlfriend was more his type, as she also liked to laze around the house all day. "You know," said the husband, "I'm sure there's enough money stashed around here for us to live pretty comfortably. If you can find it all by the time my wife returns, I'll get rid of her, and we can be together forever." The girlfriend agreed, and began to search. She had only three days in which to find all of the wife's secret hiding places.

On day one, she found a bit of money stuffed into the bottom of an old teapot, some more under a heavy canister of flour, and a few dollars held down by a polished stone above the highest kitchen shelf. Day two was more profitable: the girlfriend discovered a little leather folder of bills, which had been ingeniously taped to the bottom of a dresser drawer, as well as a face-powder tin which held nothing but cash. Working harder than she ever had in her life, she turned up stockings and coat pockets full of cash, and an old-fashioned urn that was filled to the brim with coins. She proudly showed her findings to the man, but was disappointed by his reaction.

"I'm sure there's more," he said, "but we're out of time. My wife will be home tomorrow afternoon."

"I'm not done searching," said the girlfriend, who was determined to stay in the comfortable house with all the money. The next morning she rose at dawn, and went through the house inch by inch, examining the underside of every piece of furniture and opening the seam of every stuffed cushion. She pulled pictures off the wall and peeled them out of their frames, and tore thriving plants out of their pots so that she could sift through the soil. Racing against the ticking clock, she pried up loose floorboards and emptied every carefully arranged cupboard and closet. For her efforts, she discovered only a few dollars more.

"You didn't find all the money, and what's more, you've made a big mess," complained the lazy husband. "You'd better clear it up and be on your way. My wife will be home soon to make my lunch."

"Listen," said the girlfriend, "I know I can find the rest of the money if I have more time. In the meantime, I found plenty for us to live on. Why don't you get rid of your homely wife, and everything will be all right."

The man was weak-minded and easily swayed, so he agreed. When his wife walked through the door an hour later, he was waiting inside with a hatchet. One blow to the head killed the poor woman. Her body was stuffed inside a mouldy old trunk that was found in the storage shed. Late that night, under the light of a full moon, the husband rowed out to the middle of the lake and pushed the trunk into the water. As he rowed back toward the warm lights of the house, he felt no remorse, only exhaustion. He hadn't worked so hard in years.

The next morning, the man slept late. He awoke, thinking how nice it would be to have a big breakfast of eggs and ham with some freshly brewed coffee and a thick cut of bread and butter. When he told this to his girlfriend, she only laughed. "You have a lot of work ahead of you then," she said. "For there's no bread left, and no fresh eggs or butter to be found. Also, I ate my own breakfast hours ago, and I'm not about to make another meal for you."

The man was incensed. "Then get to cleaning up this mess you made," he ordered. "The place is like a pigsty, with all of your searching for my wife's money."

"I don't feel like it" was the girlfriend's insolent reply. "In fact, I'm rather tired, and thinking of going back to bed. *You* might want to do a little cleaning, though," she suggested, then added, "and you might want to look around a bit for that big bundle of cash. It's in your best interest, too." Then she stretched like a lazy cat and wandered off to the bedroom. The man was left standing in the kitchen with no breakfast, thinking of the perfectly good wife he had just dropped into the bottom of the lake.

As the days and weeks went by, the man came to regret his actions more and more. He and his girlfriend had far too much in common to be compatible. Both were shiftless spendthrifts, so the house was quickly falling into disrepair and the money was running out. Occasionally, the two would make some small effort to find the remainder of the dead woman's wealth, but they were always unsuccessful. Frequently, they fought about the filthy state of the house and what they should do when the funds ran out.

"You should get a job," said the girlfriend.

"I didn't have one before, and I'm not getting one now," snapped the man. "You should leave, so the money that's left will last me longer."

"If I do leave, it'll be to go straight to the RCMP," the girlfriend threatened, ending the argument.

That night, the lake waters shimmered under the first full moon since the wife's murder. The husband sat out on the porch, long after his girlfriend went to bed, and regretted his actions. He did not feel guilt, exactly, or sorrow, but he felt foolish for having thrown away his comfortable lifestyle. He stared out over the water for some time, mired in self-pity. His reverie was broken when he heard a strange gurgling sound.

Bubbles began to form on the surface of the lake, and then the moonlit liquid parted. A dark form began to walk to the shore. As the thing emerged from the lake, draped in rotting weeds, the man was frozen with fear. When the dripping mass crossed the narrow strip of shore that separated the lake from the house, making sodden sounds with every step and emitting the wet stench of decay, the man's fear escalated to terror. Before she even raised her head or used one bloated, black hand to pull the weeds away from her face, he knew it was his wife.

The dead woman took one look at her husband's pathetic, shivering body and let loose a wet, bubbling laugh. Splatters of stinking water issued from her mouth as she chuckled, causing her cowardly mate to clap his hands over his eyes and moan. "Don't worry," she said, in a gurgling voice. "Despite what you did, I am here to help you. Tomorrow morning, I want you to put rat poison in that whore's coffee. Then I will return to show you where most of my money is." The wraith then turned and walked slowly back to her watery grave. The man watched, wide-eyed, until the last ripple had vanished.

The next morning, there were a number of dark, wet footprints on the bedroom floor. "What is this from?" the man asked his girlfriend. She was evasive.

"Perhaps it rained a bit. The roof might be leaking," she said, and flounced off to the kitchen. The man, who had spent a good part of the night staring at the moon and stars in a clear sky, knew it hadn't rained. Rather than pursuing the issue, though, he chose to view it as the last mess that his lazy slob of a girlfriend would ever have the opportunity to make.

The man walked into the kitchen, preparing to make the coffee as his wife had directed. He was surprised by the sight and smell of a freshly brewed pot, already sitting on the table. At his place, a cup had already been poured, and his girlfriend was stirring in sugar to sweeten it. "Let's not fight today," she suggested. "I'm making your breakfast, already, and I promise to clean up a little, after the dishes are done." The man was pleasantly surprised, but his girlfriend's change of behaviour was not enough to outweigh the promise of more money. So he thanked her, and sat down, and waited for an opportunity to put the poison in her cup.

Eventually, the girlfriend went out to the pump for some fresh water in which to boil the eggs. It only took a moment, but that was all the man needed to reach the box of rat poison, kept deep in the lowest cupboard, and stir a bit into the unsuspecting woman's coffee. He added more sugar to be safe, and was back in his chair sipping at his own cup by the time she returned.

The two drank their coffee and ate their breakfast in awkward silence. Both seemed to be preoccupied, and by the end of the meal, both were feeling ill. "I don't know what's come over me," gasped the man, as he loosened his collar and pushed his chair away from the table. Although the girlfriend was feeling unwell herself, she seemed delighted and laughed loudly.

"You're dying!" she announced. "I put poison in your coffee, you fool!" When the man gaped at her in disbelief, she offered further explanation.

"Your wife's corpse came to see me, last night," she said. "At first I was horrified, but she told me not to be afraid. You were the one who had betrayed her, she said, and if I killed you, she would show me where the rest of the money is!" The girlfriend gloated mercilessly, as the man began to sweat and clutch at his cramping stomach. She noted that her own breakfast was not sitting well— likely as a result of the excitement.

"I don't understand," the man groaned. "My wife came to see me, last night. She told me that if I killed you, the money would be mine." With great effort, he raised his head and looked into his girlfriend's eyes. "There was poison in your coffee, too," he

According to a story four generations old, there is a gruesome secret hidden beneath the shimmering waters of a lake near Fort Qu'Appelle.

wheezed, and took some pleasure in watching the woman's face grow pale with fear.

Just then, there was a sound: it was a horrid, wet shuffling that each of them remembered from the night before. The murderous pair looked up at the kitchen doorway, and were met by the terrible sight of the wife's swollen, rotting corpse. The creature opened her dripping maw to let loose a horrid laugh, and black silt trickled out and splattered on the floor.

"You double-crossed us," moaned the girlfriend, who was by then grasping at the edge of the table for support. The wraith shook her head, and her crown of sodden weeds slapped against the door frame.

"Not at all. You both have done as I requested, and now I will show you where the money is hidden." She laughed again and gestured toward the floor at her feet. There, the man and his girl-friend saw the worn, old trunk in which they had stuffed the wife's dead body. The terrible truth began to dawn on the pair as the rotting entity pulled back first the lid and then the false lining that lay within it.

There, already beginning to disintegrate from the lake water, were bundles upon bundles of bills.

Margo's grandmother always concluded by saying that it was more money than the greedy slackers could have spent in their lifetimes. Then, she would add wickedly, "Especially since they only lived for about another five minutes!"

Over the decades, Margo never forgot her grandmother's gruesomely entertaining tale. The details stayed fresh in her mind every time she thought of it and every time she told it to her own children. She has a granddaughter of her own now, too, and looks forward to the day she can tell the story to her. "Not for a few years, though," Margo laughed. "She's only four."

Someday, though, the girl will be old enough to take a drive with her grandmother, sit on the shores of Lake Qu'Appelle and hear a tale of "greed, revenge, and *murder!*" that has been heard in her family for generations.

A Tell-Tale Photograph

In the first few weeks of the year 1926, a Saskatoon mail clerk named James Johnson met a gruesome and untimely end: he was murdered with an axe. The crime was a mystery that took several days to solve. While Saskatoon police collected their evidence, one of the strangest clues showed up in the town of Indian Head, just east of Regina. It was in the form of a photograph, sent to the deceased man's brother.

The photo had been taken at James Johnson's funeral. It showed the body in its casket, surrounded by elaborate floral arrangements. As I.H. Johnson, the grieving brother, looked sorrowfully at the sombre portrait, an interesting image caught his eye. In the centre of a wreath that hung just above the dead man's head, a cluster of contrasting light and dark flowers seemed to create a silhouette. It appeared to be the head and shoulders of a woman, "as sharply defined as a cameo brooch," according to one news report. Mr. Johnson was fascinated, and began to look at the photo from various distances and angles. In every case, the silhouette of the woman was clear. When the picture was upside-down, another image emerged as well: it was the shape of a man's head, defined by the jagged interior edges of the wreath.

Mr. Johnson was astounded by the sharp and obvious images in the photo, illusions which he felt could not have been intentionally created by the florist. To confirm what he was seeing, Johnson showed the photograph to several friends and acquaintances in Indian Head. All quickly picked out the image of the woman; many also saw the man.

Was the photograph, with its strange silhouettes, relaying a significant message? Apparently so. Several days after the funeral, a woman—the wife of the late James Johnson—was taken into custody and charged with murder.

They say that dead men tell no tales, but "they" never viewed the mysterious floral arrangements at the funeral of James Johnson.

The Field

A woman named Sheila spent most of her youth on her parents' farm near Preeceville, Saskatchewan. She claims that one of her most memorable experiences from that time was a decidedly supernatural one.

"There was a little creek on the farm that my brothers and I liked to play in, in the summer," Sheila recalled. "To get to it, we'd cut across this field on our property. That field is where I saw one of the strangest things I've ever seen in my life."

Sheila was 14 years old when she witnessed the strange event. She and one of her younger brothers had been wading in the creek and had splashed each other until they were both soaking wet. When the sky clouded over and the temperature dropped, the two wanted some towels and dry clothing. They climbed through a gaping spot in the barbed wire fence and started to cut across the field. Sheila was walking a few steps ahead of her brother, and put her arm out to stop him when she saw something she didn't understand.

"Off by one edge of the field, I could see this man," she said. "I'd never seen him before, and he was dressed in really old-fashioned, frontier-style clothing. Sort of a buckskin jacket and a hat," she

How many of Saskatchewan's golden grain fields are camouflaging sinister secrets of the past?

explained. "Anyway, he had sort of a spade, or a shovel, and he was digging at this spot."

Sheila and her brother stood quietly for a few moments, watching the man and wondering if it was safe to continue across the field. Before they made their decision, something bizarre happened.

"There were no sounds at all, but all of a sudden the man dropped his shovel, and his arms went up in the air, and he sort of buckled backward as though he'd been shot from behind. Then he disappeared. I remember me and my brother just standing there with our mouths hanging open. We couldn't believe it."

No one else believed it either. When Sheila and her brother told their story at the dinner table, that night, they met nothing but scorn. "'You kids'll believe anything,' was all my Dad said," Sheila remembered. "Our other brother, he didn't believe us either, but he was a bit curious at least." The boy asked his siblings exactly where they had seen the strange scene. The next day, they were able to show him almost exactly.

"It was easy to mark," said Sheila, "because there was a big tree right in line with this guy we'd seen. I couldn't tell exactly how far away from the tree he'd been, but I knew he was exactly south of it."

The eldest of Sheila's brothers had his reasons for asking. The next day, he was out in the field with a shovel of his own, digging a small hole on the south side of the tree.

"I remember going up to him and asking him what he was up to, and he said he was looking for the treasure," Sheila laughed. "I said '*What*!' and he said 'I'm looking for whatever that guy was burying, or digging up. If he got killed over it, it must be worth something.'"

It may have been, but the boy spent the rest of the summer digging and never found a thing of value. All he had to show for his effort was a line of freshly turned earth, leading south from the large tree into the field.

"I used to tease him about it," Sheila admitted, "and he'd always say, 'You're the crazy one who thought you saw a ghost!' But I wasn't crazy. I did see it. But only that once."

Once was enough to make for a memorable summer, on one quiet Saskatchewan farm.

Her Boyfriend's Back

A certain house in Prince Albert, in which a murder had once taken place, recently sat on the real estate market for an extended period of time. It did eventually sell—to buyers who were either unaware of or unconcerned about the building's unsavoury history. A local woman named Cheryl, who knows more about the aftermath of the crime than what the newspapers ever reported, has since been wondering if the new homeowners have come to regret their decision.

"The girl who lived there before was my daughter's friend," Cheryl explained. "It was her boyfriend who was murdered in that house, and there were some very strange goings-on there after his death."

Apparently the young woman and her boyfriend had purchased the house together. They moved in and settled into their new life. Everything was going very well, and the couple intended to marry one day. Before that could happen, however, tragedy intervened.

"This girl worked as a nurse," said Cheryl, "and she worked a lot of night shifts. One night, while she was working at the hospital, her fellow had a great big party. It was one of those things that start growing and never quit, so there were a lot of people at his house that he didn't know. And they were all getting blasted flat with liquor.

"At one point, this man who was a stranger to [the homeowner] began to abuse one of the female guests. So the fellow who lived there stepped in and fought him off, and told him to get lost. But the stranger returned with a butcher knife and stabbed him. There was blood everywhere—it was a real gory kind of murder."

The young nurse was understandably devastated, and refused to return to the house for quite some time. By the time she did, she had moved on with her life and was seeing another man. When the other man moved into the house with her, though, mysterious events began to take place.

"Often, she would be in bed, and she'd feel someone shaking her shoulder. Like someone trying to shake her awake. But when she'd open her eyes, no one would be there. And there were other times when she'd hear her former boyfriend calling her name throughout the house. But she could never track him down."

Through her daughter, Cheryl heard a number of stories about paranormal things that were happening in that home. And she learned that the ghost's attention was not focused exclusively upon the young woman.

"The fellow who was living with this girl, whenever he'd try to hug or kiss her, he'd feel this column of cold, cold air rush past him. And sometimes he'd even feel something slap him across the face."

The young woman was unable to cope with having both a flesh-and-blood man and a spirit vying for her attentions. It wasn't long before she moved out and put the house up for sale. What would be interesting to know is whether the ghost of the boyfriend, who was so attached to her, moved right along with the woman or remained in the house in which he died.

Only the young woman, and the new owners of the house, know for sure—and they might be unwilling to say.

A STRANGE ASSORTMENT

*Ghosts can be unpredictable,
so there are many stories that refuse
to fit into tidy categories.
Equally frustrating is the fact that
while searching for tales about spirits,
one will inevitably encounter a few
strange-but-true accounts of other
paranormal phenomena which,
while not exactly ghostly,
are too good to leave out.*

*Here are the eerie extras that have
been woven into Saskatchewan's rich
tapestry of supernatural legends.*

The Four-Minute Dream

The world is filled with mysteries, and we human beings need look no further than our own minds to find the most fascinating of them. In 1964, a man named J.H. Grant from Harlan, Saskatchewan, wrote to the *News of the North* about an amazing experience that he had had.

Grant recalled an event that took place many years earlier. He had just put in a day of hard labour on a threshing crew at a neighbour's farm, and then had walked three miles back to his own home. Grant was looking forward to having dinner with his wife and small sons, so he hadn't eaten with the rest of the crew. By the time he walked into his kitchen, he was weak with fatigue and hunger.

"There was a roaring fire in the kitchen stove, with chickens roasting in the oven, but my wife and the boys were evidently out around the buildings somewhere," Grant wrote. He decided to take the opportunity to rest a little and warm himself by the stove. As he pulled up a comfortable chair and sat down, Grant glanced at the clock on the kitchen wall. It read ten minutes to six. "I must have dropped off to sleep at once," he recalled. The farmer was then immediately drawn into the most vivid and detailed dream that he would ever have.

It began with Grant's wife coming into the kitchen and the couple having what he would later describe as a "peculiar argument." Seething with anger, the man stormed out to the barn and hooked up a team of horses. He then drove out of the farmyard to the school house some miles away for a community supper. When he arrived at his destination, however, Grant was mortified to see that he had forgotten his trousers, and had to turn his rig around and return home.

During the return trip to the farm, Grant dreamed that he became hopelessly lost on the previously familiar roads. Eventually, he found himself in a small town that was nearly 15 miles away from his home.

Grant was then suddenly travelling on foot. "Distinctly I remembered walking every step of the way, seeing landmarks, checking my direction against the stars, smelling the alkali water of a lake that I knew, hearing frogs croaking and so on." Somewhere along the way, he dreamed that his foot became caught in a railway track, as a locomotive bore down on him. With a tremendous effort, Grant managed to pull himself free. He fell backward, landing on the ground with a hard thud that jarred him out of the dream.

Grant opened his eyes and found himself in his own kitchen, in the chair by the stove, watching his wife adjust the gas lamp that she had just lighted. It was the light of the lamp that had seemed to be the headlight of the oncoming train. Grant felt that he must have slept the evening away, and looked up at the clock. He was stunned to note that it read six minutes before six: since he had sat down, only four minutes had passed.

It was difficult to believe the complexity of the dream that he had just experienced in such a brief amount of time. After supper, while the whole thing was still clear in his memory, Grant sat down to record all the vivid details that he recalled. The resulting account filled six typewritten pages.

The strange episode remained fascinating to J.H. Grant for all his life. He would always wonder about the perplexing aspects of time and how, "under certain conditions, time [can seem] so different from what we are accustomed to…"

A Scene Out of Time

For someone who researches ghost stories, there are always those few tales that seem impossible to pin down. They tend to intrigue and frustrate in equal measure. One legend, from the area around the Battlefords, has been told to me by several people, although no one has actually witnessed the phenomenon. It is well worth sharing, anyway.

According to folklore, there is a rural area outside the Battlefords where one will come across a clearing which is defined by a circle of trees. If you happen to walk through the foliage and into the grassy field, a strange event will be triggered that could best be described as a shift in time.

First, the quality of the air seems to change. Then comes a shimmering in the centre of the clearing, and a ghostly image begins to take shape. It is said that if you watch long enough, the image solidifies into a very real-looking scene. There is a covered wagon, a team of horses, and a family wearing 19th-century pioneer clothing. The people are always oblivious to whomever has joined them in their camp, and simply go about their business. They build a small cookfire, take utensils and supplies out of the back of the wagon and prepare a meal. When the food is ready, they sit down to eat. When they have finished eating, the scene disappears by becoming increasingly insubstantial and then fading into thin air.

Is this a timewarp, or a haunting? With so little information, it's difficult to say. There are cases on record of a rare phenomenon known as retrocognition, or post-cognition—literally, "backward knowing." People who experience it report that their surroundings abruptly change to a scene from the past. As opposed to someone who sees a ghost who appears displaced in the present time, witnesses of retrocognition seem to be the ones transported back through the years or even centuries.

Likely the most famous of all retrocognitive experiences was documented by two English academics, Anne Moberly and Eleanor Jourdain, in their book, *An Adventure*, which was published in 1911. In it, they wrote of the vacation they had taken ten years earlier in Versailles. During a strange walk to the Petit Trianon, where the last royal occupant had been the doomed queen, Marie Antoinette, both women saw characters and settings that were later determined to have existed in the final days leading up to the French Revolution.

With nothing but trees and sky as a backdrop, however, it is more difficult to determine an approximate era and argue for retrocognition in the Battlefords case. But the situation does provide interesting food for thought which applies to any ghost story: is the apparition displaced in the observer's time, or has the observer travelled briefly backward through the veil of years to witness events in their own day?

It's something worth thinking about—perhaps while hiking about the Saskatchewan wilderness, looking for a very special circular clearing in the trees.

The Masefield Cult of Three

Just before the outbreak of the First World War, two English brothers named Sid and Archie Chandler set out to make lives for themselves in Canada. The brothers settled in the small farming community of Masefield, south of Swift Current. With the benefit of a stake from their well-do-do family back in Britain as well as a good education and fine work ethic, the men prospered. For more than a decade they concentrated on building up their successful agricultural operation and became two of the most influential people in the area. Then, in 1927, the Chandlers changed their focus from farming to Armageddon.

Archie and Sid had become convinced that the prophecies of the Bible were about to be fulfilled. Eager to share their conviction with their neighbours, they erected a large tent in the rolling southern hills and began preaching about preparedness for the second coming of Christ. Their evident sincerity attracted a number of followers at first, but as the predicted doomsday date came and went without incident, the once-faithful drifted away.

The Chandlers—Archie, Sid, and Sid's wife—were the only remaining members of the cult by the fall of 1929. Their beliefs were unshaken, however, and they chose a new date upon which to focus. November 6, 1929, was to be "The Last Day," and the brothers decided to abandon their worldly ways completely in order to make better preparations. Their land, stock and equipment were all sold. The three Chandlers, along with Sid's two small children, moved into the tent that had once been used for sermons. On this camping ground, they stored ten tons of flour and 3000 bushels of rolled oats, and waited for the end.

As the Chandlers counted down the days, their tiny cult and strong beliefs became an item of national interest. The *Regina Leader-Post* reported that "their tented home, amid a sea of hills, [had become] the centre of attraction to travellers from far and near." The Canadian Press News Service even carried the story, from coast to coast. When November 6, 1929, passed without incident, though, the Chandlers immediately became old news. As author John Robert Colombo pointed out in his book *Mysterious Canada*, no member of the media bothered to interview the Chandlers on "Doomsday Plus One."

Mysterious Music

In the fall of 1999, a woman named Ruth Peck, from Pilot Butte in southeastern Saskatchewan, wrote to *FATE* magazine about a purchase she had made at an estate sale.

It was a simple pottery mug, decorated with a pattern of musical notes. The mug had originally been a novelty item, designed to play a tune when it was picked up and to stop when it was set back down. The musical mechanism no longer worked, but the cup was pretty, so Ruth thought she might use it to store pens and pencils. Ruth Peck bought the no-longer-musical mug, along with a number of other items.

Shortly thereafter, Ruth was awakened early one morning by the somewhat mechanical, tinkling sound of music. She got out of bed and tried to track down the source of the tune, but it had stopped once her feet were on the floor. Ruth thought little of it until the next morning, when she was roused by the same mysterious melody. In fact, the music awakened her several mornings in a row before she was able to pinpoint the source. It was the pottery mug, which sat cheerfully on a kitchen shelf, displaying its supposedly-silent motif of musical notes.

Ruth tried to make the mug play its tune, by lifting it, shaking it, and even jumping on the floor to cause it to vibrate. Nothing worked. Every morning at precisely ten minutes before seven, however, the tiny chimes played a version of "You Light Up My Life." That is to say, the mug played if Ruth was still asleep at that time. If she had already risen, it remained silent.

One day while shopping, Ruth happened to meet the woman who had organized the estate sale. She was the daughter of the man who had once owned the melodious piece of pottery. Ruth said nothing of her strange purchase, but very casually asked the lady if her father had been in the habit of rising at 6:50 AM. The woman looked stricken and gasped, "No, but that was the exact time he died!" She then turned and left before Ruth could say another word.

Ruth Peck decided to keep her mysterious, musical mug, despite its practice of waking her so early. When she does want to sleep in now, she talks to the mug, telling it the night before not to wake her. Making such requests has proven to be only half effective, however. "Sometimes it complies, sometimes not," says Ruth. "It certainly seems to have a mind of its own."

The Freshest Flowers

In a modest, small-town cemetery in southern Saskatchewan, there is one grave site that stands out for the strangest of reasons. The marker is nondescript, and only a handful of people would recognize the name that is upon it. Whenever a bouquet of flowers is respectfully placed there, however, it stays fresh for a remarkably long time.

A former caretaker at the cemetery remembered the inexplicable phenomenon. "When I'd been working there about two weeks, someone came in and set a nice little bunch of fresh flowers at the base of the headstone. I don't know what they were... they smelled nice. Anyway, every couple of days, I'd take a walk around the place and check for floral arrangements that were turning bad. I'd toss them out, when they did. And every time I'd go by this little bunch of flowers, they looked as good as the first day they were there. After a week, I checked to see if they were artificial, but they weren't. After three weeks, I was cutting a bit of a wide berth around the grave, because I just didn't know what to make of it."

The man wondered if the flowers hadn't been replaced with an identical arrangement when he wasn't looking, but was fairly certain they had not. Eventually, he asked the previous caretaker, who happened to be an old friend, about the grave. The friend accepted the story with a nod and seemed not the least bit surprised.

"He told me, 'That's just the way it is on that grave. When she gets flowers, don't even bother checking them for a month or two. They just stay fresh.'"

The caretaker worked at that cemetery for more than three years. In that time, he found the strange phenomenon to be absolutely consistent, and never discovered a logical explanation.

There is one grave in Saskatchewan where a gift of fresh flowers will remain fresh—for an extraordinarily long time.

A Cure That Could Kill

In the spring of 1937, the *Regina Leader-Post* ran an article in which it was reported that witchcraft was alive and well in the province of Saskatchewan. According to the account, the craft had changed, however. "The occult lore is not used to inflict harm on enemies, as the vindictive hags of the past tried to do," declared the paper. "Modern witchcraft seeks to cure ailments of the body," the article went on to say, suggesting that witches of the day were more likely to be classified as "helpful hags."

A few "secrets of the art" were given away in the story. It was said that for stomach troubles, water in which charred wood had been soaked was a certain remedy. Curing cramps was more complicated: one had to take a large pot filled with corn and cutlery and bring it to a boil. The broth was not the cure, however. Nor was the corn. To bring about relief, the full pot was to be placed on the patient's stomach.

One prairie witch happened to do more harm than good when she tried to help an ailing woman from Sturgis. The woman had been suffering terrible pains after lifting a heavy boiler full of laundry. On the advice of friends, she sought treatment from an aged and supposedly powerful witch who lived just outside the town.

The old woman began by performing a diagnostic test. In a room where the lamp was turned down low, she muttered a series of strange phrases and poured melted beeswax into a pot of cold water. She explained that the shapes which formed would tell them what was physically wrong with the woman and what must be done. Both women watched in awed silence as the wax drippings began to harden into shapes. Then suddenly the witch spoke.

"I see a grave and mourners," she announced. Then, perhaps needlessly, the crone explained to her patient that death was imminent, and that nothing could be done. It goes without saying that this particular alternative treatment did nothing to help the patient. In fact, according to the *Leader-Post*, it resulted in a fairly serious setback: "Frightened by the prophecy, the ailing woman became so ill that she had to be taken to the Preeceville hospital. She is now at home recovering from the effects of back strain and witchcraft."

The poor woman learned that, even with the most highly recommended witches, it is always wise to get a second opinion.

The Moose Jaw Tunnels

One of the most fascinating historical facts and greatest tourist draws belonging to the city of Moose Jaw was officially denied for more than 75 years. It might have still been under wraps today, had not an unfortunate accident befallen a motorist on Main Street. The man was driving along, when suddenly the pavement collapsed beneath him. The driver found himself trapped in a deep hole, and the city fathers found themselves admitting to a decades-old secret: beneath the city of Moose Jaw, there existed a network of tunnels which told the story of the small prairie city's unsavoury past.

Today, the reluctance to talk about the tunnels has vanished. What was once considered Moose Jaw's "dirty laundry" is now seen as being worthy of promotion. A portion of the underground maze has been restored and opened to tourists. More than 100,000 visitors have paid to follow a guide around the subterranean network that is billed as "the Tunnels of Little Chicago." More than 100,000 visitors have heard the strange stories of how it came to be—and, eventually, what it came to be.

It all began in 1908, a dark time in Canada's history, when hysterical fear of the "yellow peril" led to many hate crimes against the Chinese. In Moose Jaw's CPR rail yards, several railway workers were ruthlessly beaten by whites who believed that the Chinese men were taking their jobs. This ever-present physical threat, combined with the economic one created by Ottawa when it imposed its infamous head tax on Chinese immigrants, literally drove the workers underground. A number of secret tunnels were dug. They were meant to provide a temporary place for the Chinese workers to hide until the volatile situation improved. At the time, no one could have guessed how permanent this underground community would become.

The men made themselves as comfortable as possible, and eventually brought women to live with them in their unusual underground habitat. Unbelievably, children were even born and raised there. The tunnel community developed a way of life that showed high levels of determination and resourcefulness. Winter temperatures were made bearable by the fact that the rooms were built next to the heated basements of above-ground structures. Entrances to the maze were in the basements of buildings owned by legal Chinese immigrants. The underground residents often worked for laundries and restaurants which were owned by these sympathizers. Their payment was usually food and other supplies which would be taken below-ground to the dark, rat-infested, makeshift homes.

The tunnels were used for many years in this way. By the 1920s, when the Chinese families had moved out, they came to serve another purpose. It was the days of Prohibition, and Moose Jaw had been pinpointed as an ideally situated bootlegging hub.

The little city was a major CPR terminus and was connected to the United States by the Soo Line, so shipping the illegal whiskey was easy. Certain individuals also recognized that Moose Jaw's corrupt police force and remote location made it the perfect place to hide from the U.S. law. Before long, the city was visited regularly by members of the Chicago mob, including the notorious Al Capone. Needless to say, the potential usefulness of the existing underground tunnel network was not lost on the wily gangsters.

Before long, the tunnels were being used for gambling, prostitution and warehousing illegal booze. One dark corridor led directly to a shed in the rail yards, where a shipment could be loaded or unloaded from a train car, safely away from prying eyes.

Today, there are still some residents of Moose Jaw who have memories of the city's secret underground. An 89-year-old man named Laurence Mullin has a repertoire of stories about working as a newspaper boy on the streets and as a messenger boy beneath them. A woman named Nancy Gray recalls her late father, a barber named Bill Beamish, being summoned to the tunnels several times to cut Al Capone's hair. There are men who remember as boys meeting a Capone crony named Diamond Jim Grady. Grady, who was described as having eyes like a reptile, would always advise his young admirers to stay on the straight and narrow.

After the Chicago mob vacated Moose Jaw, the tunnels became a dirty secret that city officials were eager to keep hidden beneath the city streets. For decades, they succeeded. No secret keeps forever, though, which has proven to be for the best, in this case. Moose Jaw's strangest feature became its most interesting one, when a decades-old, underground mystery first saw the light of day.

The Out-of-Body Afternoon

In 1952, a woman named Adelaide Weese was living with her husband William in Weyburn, Saskatchewan. One day in the spring of that year, William decided to spend a day off visiting his brother, who lived in a small town some distance away. This plan suited Adelaide; knowing she would be alone for the day, she planned to start her spring housecleaning.

The Weeses rose at dawn that day. William caught the early train, and Adelaide immediately tackled her cleaning projects. The hardwood floors were waxed and polished to a high shine. Walls were scrubbed clean of the winter's grime, and cupboards were systematically emptied, washed, and reorganized. Adelaide went through buckets of soapy water and dozens of rags throughout the morning. By lunchtime, she was exhausted, and decided to lie down for a rest.

No sooner had Adelaide made herself comfortable on the soft, quilted coverlet of her double bed than she began to feel a strange sensation. Suddenly she was as light as a feather and floating upwards. She had risen all the way to the bedroom ceiling when a disembodied voice made a startling announcement. "You are dead," it boomed. As the words echoed in the room, Adelaide looked down at the bed. There, she could see her pale and seemingly lifeless body. She was filled with fear and concern for her husband. Her first thought was of the terrible shock that William would suffer when he returned from his trip to find her dead.

The minutes ticked by, and when nothing further happened, Adelaide began to experiment with her new "form." She found that she could float into the other rooms of the house, despite the fact that she was bound to her physical body by a silver cord. The further she travelled, the thinner the cord became, stretching to cover the distance. Adelaide drifted into the living room, watching the silver band become no thicker than a strand of fine wire. She was busy marvelling at that when a truck pulled up in front of the house.

Through the living room window, Adelaide saw a delivery man carrying a large package up the front walk. She remembered that she had arranged to have McKinnon's Department Store deliver a bookcase that afternoon. As the man knocked on the door, however, Adelaide found that she was unable either to open the door or speak to the fellow. Fortunately, he thought to try the back door, which had been left unlocked. The man poked his head into the kitchen and called out, "Is anyone home?" Adelaide was floating no more than a few feet in front of his face, but it was obvious that he could not see her. The man pulled the bookcase into the middle of the kitchen and left, having made his delivery.

Not long after, Adelaide felt herself being slowly pulled back into the bedroom. As she drew closer to her body, the connecting cord became thicker and darker in colour. Then, as suddenly as it began, the experience was over. Adelaide felt and saw nothing more for some time.

When she awoke, it was in a cold sweat. She tried to get out of bed, but was so weak, she collapsed back onto the pillows. It was half an hour before she felt able to rise. During that time, while Adelaide lay on the bed regaining her strength, she looked at the clock and made a few calculations. By her best estimate, she had been floating around her home for more than an hour.

As Adelaide finally managed to walk shakily out of the bedroom, there was another knocking at the back door. A neighbour had come to borrow some pastry flour. The woman took one look at Adelaide's pale face and asked if she was ill. For a moment, that made perfect sense to Adelaide. Perhaps she had been ill: perhaps she had been suffering from a fever that had caused a wild hallucination. But as she turned into the kitchen to fetch the flour, she realized that she had not been dreaming, for there, in the middle of the kitchen floor, was the bookcase that she had seen delivered. Years later, Adelaide Weese would write, "From this detail I knew it had not been a dream or my imagination, but I truly had been out of my body."

In Saskatchewan Skies

They say that "the truth is out there," and it appears that "they" might just be talking about Saskatchewan. Apparently, a province that has so many crops in which to draw circles is very appealing to alien life forms. There have been numerous UFO sightings and encounters in Saskatchewan over the years. They range from laughable to believable, and from mundane to truly fascinating. These are a few of the more interesting ones I came across, while searching for the province's ghost lore.

* * *

Nipawin, Summer of 1933
Two men and one woman abandoned their pickup to follow a mysterious bright orange glow that was coming from deep within the woods. They reported that the source of the glow was a large

oval-shaped object that was domed at the top and rounded underneath. They also claimed to have seen approximately a dozen human-like creatures in silver uniforms busily performing repairs to the craft. The witnesses said that when they returned to the site two days later, they found large, square impressions in the earth that they were certain had been left by the "legs" of the UFO. Photos of the impressions were taken with a small brownie box camera. No authorities or publications were interested in the pictures at the time, however, and they were eventually lost.

Regina, July 1947

E.G. Bannister and his wife reported seeing what they considered to be a "flying saucer" while driving along the Trans-Canada Highway. It was shaped like a dinner plate and appeared to be moving at a fair rate of speed and at an altitude of about 2000 feet. On the same evening, similar sightings were reported in Indian Head and Saskatoon.

Dundurn, March 1950

"A flying thing, not shaped like a saucer, shot across the sky," was the description Bill Evans provided of his UFO sighting. The object appeared to Evans and his wife to be travelling southeast at a height of about 1000 feet. The couple was able to make out "a light, and what looked like exhaust," but the object's shape was not distinguishable.

Regina, June 1950

Mr. and Mrs. H. Wilks witnessed a strange, crescent-shaped object soaring over the northwest section of the city. The leading edge of the object was outlined by a dull glow. According to Mr. Wilks, the object travelled in a northwesterly direction for about

20 seconds before turning south and then east. The UFO, which had been travelling quite slowly and occasionally stopping to hover, then increased its speed and vanished.

Regina, April 1952

At 3:30 AM one Friday morning, Mrs. N. Gataint awoke to see a strange object moving across the sky in a southwesterly direction. She said that it had "a tail like a kite," was shaped like a dinner plate, and flew at quite a low altitude. "It stood still for a few seconds, then shot out spurts of fire and moved on." Trans Canada Airlines said that a North Star aircraft travelling from Calgary to Winnipeg passed over the city at 3:30 that same morning. The craft had flashing identifying lights on each wing tip, and on its tail.

Island Falls, August 1952

A mysterious flying object emitting a vapor trail was seen travelling toward the White Sands Dam and back. The lone witness claimed that the UFO made no sound and eventually vanished into the clear, blue sky.

Lake Alma, December 1958

Three people reported that a kite-shaped object had been moving through the sky very slowly at a high altitude. As the object travelled toward the east, it glowed first blue and then red. A few minutes later, it sped upwards and out of sight.

Saskatoon, September 1963

A young girl was admitted to hospital, suffering from shock, after she and three playmates saw a bright oval object drop something into a field. When the children approached the site, they were greeted by a nine-foot-tall man, dressed in white monks' robes, who gestured toward them and made unintelligible sounds.

Invermay, May 1966

A bright light was seen travelling across the sky by seven different people. At one point, the light stopped and remained in place for five full minutes. It then climbed rapidly out of sight.

Harptree, August 1966

A single witness reported seeing a brilliant globe of light in the northern sky. The light hung in the air for approximately 30 seconds, then zoomed directly toward the witness before flying up into the clouds.

Shaunavon, July 1967

Evelyn Brown snapped two photos of a flying "disc-shaped" object near her farmhouse. The pictures were denounced as fakes, prior to their scheduled publication in a European magazine, but Brown maintained that they were genuine.

Saskatchewan's huge sky has been the backdrop of many UFO sightings.

Regina, August 1968

A Canadian Forces Hercules C-130E was flying over Regina during a routine flight, when the eight-man crew observed a "dirigible-shaped" craft. The UFO appeared to have five or six dark rectangular patches on its side, no gondola or tail, and emitted no contrail. It was visible to the crew for approximately 90 seconds, then it shrank rapidly in size and disappeared quickly into the southwest. All eight crew members agreed upon the description of the craft and this version of events.

Duval, June 1968

Martin Bouelen was walking outside, alone, at midnight, when he saw a large egg-shaped object hovering in the sky. The object, which was in sight for five to ten minutes, was a dark mass which blotted out the stars. Bouelen added that it had "white, frosted Christmas-tree lights" at one end.

Arcola, December 1968

Harvey Holloway reported seeing a large mushroom-shaped object travelling across the sky toward the northwest. Holloway was alone, and said the sighting lasted for five to seven seconds.

Balcarres, November 1973

Sergeant Jack Briscoe of the RCMP was responding to a call about some mysterious lights over a farmer's field. He arrived at the sight to find a bright, mushroom-shaped object bouncing around the field. He later described the object as being about 50 metres in diameter, and floating 30 metres above the ground. It appeared orange to those closest to it, and purple to those who were farther away. Along the UFO were banks of lights which flashed red and orange. Another officer on the scene reported that through a rifle scope, he was able to see portholes on the side of the object.

There were other strange happenings in the same area on the same day. One man snapped a photo of a mysterious object hovering over a nearby field. Another reported that his truck had broken down for no apparent reason, just after he had seen a strange object flying overhead. Mechanics at a local garage later told him that the electrical system had melted. Yet a third person lost his home to a fire that he claimed was set by an inexplicable craft which flew over it.

This remains one of the most mysterious cases ever filed with the National Research Council.

Langenburg, September 1974

Edwin Fuhr, a canola farmer, was working in a field when he encountered five dome-shaped, metallic objects. They were hovering a few inches above the ground, and appeared to be revolving. Fuhr could see that one of them was "probing around in the grass." Suddenly, the objects rose about two hundred feet in the air, stopped spinning, and emitted downward blasts of vapour, before speeding away. The vapour blasts left behind five perfectly round rings of flattened canola in Fuhr's field. The RCMP report noted that the circles had to have been caused by something "exerting what had to be heavy air or exhaust pressure over the high grass."

Weyburn, January 1977

Bea Holdstock reported seeing a number of brilliant, bouncing lights near her farm. When she returned home later she found her living room in total disarray. Furniture had been overturned, and the draperies were damaged beyond repair. Four nights after the strange event, Holdstock was sleeping on the living-room sofa when she was awakened by a bright light, which appeared and disappeared three times. The woman later said there was no accompanying sound, but "a feeling of electricity in the air."

Mossbank, March 1987

The Cullen family was travelling from Regina to Gravelbourg, when Susan Cullen looked to her right and saw a bright object, "about 12 feet in length with a dome on top," keeping pace with the car. She described the object as being approximately "a telephone pole and a half away and about the height of a telephone pole" above the ground. Susan and her husband Charlie then both witnessed the object move ahead of their vehicle, and take off into the distance at an incredible speed.

Langenburg, October 1989

There were two separate UFO sightings within two days near this southeastern town of 1400 people. On October 11, a group of high school students and two teachers reported watching a brightly lighted object in the sky for a period of ten to 15 minutes. On October 13, a woman named Rose Neumeier watched for as long as five minutes as a huge, silvery craft silently floated over her farmyard. "I was scared at first, and curious," Neumeier said. "You're transfixed."

The province's broad expanses of grain have often acted as a canvas for the extraterrestrial art commonly referred to as "crop circles."

Milestone, August 1992

A farmer named Joe Rennick discovered a strange 60- by 20-foot depression in his wheat field. He said that it looked as though "something big had bounced a couple of times across the crop." The wheat had been flattened and swirled in three-foot-wide spirals, and the normally soft soil had become rock-hard. Even stranger, however, was what Rennick found on top of the wheat— a dead, flat porcupine.

The animal had been flattened to a thickness of about two inches. There was no blood around the animal, and no tears to its flesh. Other than being only two inches thick, the animal seemed "undamaged." Rennick left it in the field for three weeks under the hot summer sun. When the porcupine showed no signs of decomposing, the farmer eventually threw its carcass away.

Rocanville, September 1996

In a field close to Rocanville, two nearly perfect circles of flattened wheat were discovered. The circles were approximately 45 feet in diameter. The stalks of wheat had been bent to the ground in a neat spiral pattern, but not broken, and the ground itself showed no sign of compression. An Esterhazy man named Daniel Clairmont, who investigated the case in his spare time, said that such occurrences were more common in southeastern Saskatchewan than anyone would suspect. "They're happening all over the place, but most people don't want to report them," Clairmont was quoted as saying.

Spy Hill, September 1998

Joe DeCorby was swathing a wheat field near his home when he made a startling discovery. It was a crop circle, 24 feet in diameter, fitting the description of two such circles discovered in Rocanville two years earlier. The wheat stalks inside the circle were bent close to the ground and lay in a tightly woven, counter-clock-wise pattern. Stalks standing a fraction of an inch outside the circle remained straight and untouched. DeCorby discounted any theory that the circle could have been a man-made hoax. He said that the effect was much too precise, and the wheat field was so ripe that anyone moving through it would have left obvious signs.

* * *

According to researchers who are experts on the subject of UFOs, this collection is but a tiny sample of the documented sightings in Saskatchewan. Apparently, in this province, those who wish to witness something extraordinary need do no more than keep their eyes on the sky.

ENJOY MORE HAUNTING TALES IN LONE PINE PUBLISHING'S "GHOST STORIES" SERIES!

The colourful history of North America includes many spine-tingling tales of the super-natural. Lone Pine's ghost stories research and reveal the rich diversity of haunted places on the continent. Our ghostly tales involve well-known theatres, buildings and other landmarks, many of which are still in use. Collect the whole series!

Ghost Stories of Manitoba
by Barbara Smith
the Virgin Mary at Cross Lake • Winnipeg's Walker Theatre • the Manitoba Theatre Centre • the old Masonic Temple
$14.95 Cdn • ISBN 1-55105-180-X • 5.25" X 8.25" • 240 pages

More Ghost Stories of Alberta
by Barbara Smith
Fort Edmonton Park's Firkins House • Calgary's Old City Hall • the Fort Saskatchewan Jail • Jasper Park Lodge
$14.95 Cdn • ISBN 1-55105-083-8 • 5.25" X 8.25" • 232 pages

Ontario Ghost Stories
by Barbara Smith
a gangster hideout near Muskoka • Dundurn Castle in Hamilton • the farm of the murdered Donnellys • Canada's Hockey Hall of Fame
$14.95 Cdn • ISBN 1-55105-203-2 • 5.25" X 8.25" • 240 pages

Ghost Stories of Hollywood
by Barbara Smith
Griffith Park • Mann's Chinese Theater • John Wayne's haunted yacht • major movie studios and more
$14.95 US • ISBN 1-55105-241-5 • 5.25" X 8.25" • 224 pages

Ghost Stories of California
by Barbara Smith
Alcatraz • the Queen Mary • a historic Tinseltown hotel • the Joshua Tree Inn and more
$14.95 Cdn • ISBN 1-55105-237-7 • 5.25" X 8.25" • 224 pages

Ghost Stories of the Rocky Mountains
by Barbara Smith
Banff Springs Hotel • Denver's Unsinkable Molly Brown • the Frank Slide • Warren Air Force Base and more
$14.95 Cdn 1-55105-165-6 • 5.25" X 87.25" • 240 pages

Ghost Stories of Washington
by Barbara Smith
Seattle Underground • Yakima's Capitol Theatre • Port Townsend's Manresa Castle • Gonzaga University and more
$14.95 Cdn • ISBN 1-55105-260-1 • 5.25" X 8.25" • 232 pages

These and other Ghost Stories books are available at your local bookseller or order direct from Lone Pine Publishing at 1-800-661-9017.